D0743501

The Q Guide to

Designing Women

For my Queen
Tava.
the real Designing Women
with much
love,
Allen

The Q Guides

FROM ALYSON BOOKS

AVAILABLE NOW:

THE Q GUIDE TO THE GOLDEN GIRLS
by Jim Colucci

THE Q GUIDE TO SOAP OPERAS
by Daniel R. Coleridge

THE Q GUIDE TO BROADWAY
by Seth Rudetsky

THE Q GUIDE TO OSCAR PARTIES
(AND OTHER AWARD SHOWS)
by Joel Perry

THE Q GUIDE TO FIRE ISLAND
by Steve Weinstein

THE Q GUIDE TO AMSTERDAM
by Dara Colwell

THE Q GUIDE TO NYC PRIDE
by Patrick Hinds

THE Q GUIDE TO WINE AND COCKTAILS
by Scott & Scott

THE Q GUIDE TO CLASSIC MONSTER MOVIES
by Douglas McEwan

THE Q GUIDE TO DESIGNING WOMEN
by Allen Crowe

COMING SOON:

THE Q GUIDE TO GAY BEACHES
by David Allyn

THE Q GUIDE TO BUFFY THE VAMPIRE SLAYER
by Gregory L. Norris

POP CULTURE

Q

OUT THERE

GUIDE

The Q Guide to

Designing Women

**Stuff You Didn't Even Know You Wanted
to Know** . . . about Julia, Mary Jo,
Charlene, Suzanne, and the beloved sitcom

[**Allen Crowe**]

alyson books
N E W Y O R K

© 2007 BY ALLEN CROWE
ALL RIGHTS RESERVED

MANUFACTURED IN THE UNITED STATES OF AMERICA

THIS TRADE PAPERBACK ORIGINAL IS PUBLISHED BY
ALYSON BOOKS
245 WEST 17TH STREET
NEW YORK, NY 10011

DISTRIBUTION IN THE UNITED KINGDOM BY
TURNAROUND PUBLISHER SERVICES LTD.
UNIT 3, OLYMPIA TRADING ESTATE
COBURG ROAD, WOOD GREEN
LONDON N22 6TZ ENGLAND

FIRST EDITION: NOVEMBER 2007

07 08 09 10 11 a 10 9 8 7 6 5 4 3 2 1

ISBN: 1-59530-036-X
ISBN-13: 978-1-59350-036-8

LIBRARY OF CONGRESS CATALOGING-IN-PUBLICATION DATA
ARE ON FILE.

COVER DESIGN BY VICTOR MINGOVITS

This book is lovingly dedicated
to
Gale MacNeill and Michael Knee,
whose friendship outshines the Designing Women's,
and to
Linda Bloodworth Thomason,
for giving me something to talk about
in the first place.

Contents

On the set of *Designing Women* following the filming of
season three finale episode "Julia Drives Over the First
Amendment." (Front row, left to right) Delta Burke, Annie
Potts, Jean Smart. (Back row, left to right) Meshach Taylor,
The Q Guide to Designing Women author Allen Crowe,
Dixie Carter. (Photo from author's personal collection)

Introduction

ON AUGUST 12, 1987, I HAD BEEN living in Los Angeles less than two months. I had left behind six years of school teaching in inner-city Atlanta and still had a few weeks to go before beginning what would be three years of school teaching in Los Angeles. In the entire City of Angels, I knew three people and I was living in an apartment I was afraid to leave after dark. (Since the rent was only $525 a month, I decided to view my next-door neighbor's arrest as good story material and save for a better place as if my life probably depended on it.)

I had come to California to pursue my dream of writing for television. (Buddy and Sally made it look so easy.) I was still young enough, or foolish enough, to be shocked that no one was waiting with open arms to put me on their writing staff. As a matter of fact, you weren't considered a writer worth hiring unless you had an agent and agents weren't interested in representing you unless you could get work. It made for exciting tail chasing. I started filling my days (cheaply) by attending tapings of television sitcoms. I saw them all: *Cheers, 227, The Facts of Life, The Golden Girls, 9 to 5, Mama's Family,* even *Women in Prison.* (Who could resist the opportunity to see Peggy Cass, the original Agnes Gooch from the Rosalind Russell version of *Auntie Mame*?)

On this particular Thursday in August, I was taking in the first taping of the second season of a show I had already discovered, *Designing Women.* The episode, written by Linda Bloodworth Thomason, was called "Killing All the Right People" and dealt head-on with homophobia and the AIDS crisis. By the time the last scene was shot, I was completely hooked on the show.

When the following Thursday rolled around, I found myself once again in line to join the studio audience. It became part of my weekly routine. (College friends teased me that I was in danger of becoming the Mrs. Miller of *Designing Women*—an obscure reference to the little ol' lady who never missed a *Merv Griffin Show*.) By the middle of September, I had made friends with a couple of the show's production assistants; I was acting like a part of the *Designing Women* team. I felt I was just doing my part when, during the filming of an episode featuring Alice Ghostley called "Half an Air Bubble Off," I noticed that a previously established character was being called by a different name. I've always had a mind for useless trivia. I called over my new PA friend and explained the mistake. She looked at me like I was half an air bubble off myself, but shared the information with Harry Thomason, series executive producer and the director of the episode, who had someone check. Fortunately, I was correct.

The following week, when I arrived for the show, my PA friend told me Harry would like to see me in an office down on the stage. I'd like to claim I immediately thought I was being offered a writing job, but in reality I figured I was going to be told to stop stalking the show. Harry asked me a few questions, mostly about what I was doing to pay the bills (teaching junior high) and what I wanted to do (write for television). By the end of the meeting, I was the official keeper of continuity for the show. (Not that I was always successful: Carlene's name came out of nowhere. Why she couldn't have been Marlene, Harlene, or Darlene, I'll never understand.)

From that night until the final show was filmed in 1993, I only missed one other episode in the show's seven-season run due to a death in my immediate family. For me, *Designing Women* was a magic combination of brilliant writer and world-class cast. Ultimately, I sold my first script to *Hearts Afire* and have been on the writing staffs of *Evening Shade* and HBO's *12 Miles of Bad Road*. I have also had a couple of my plays produced. Still, I will always regret that I was never fortunate enough to write an episode of *Designing Women*. I hope that this book will, in some small way, help me get it out of my system!

Allen Crowe, June 2007

The Q Guide to
Designing Women

Linda Bloodworth Thomason discusses a scene with the cast. (Left to right) Linda Bloodworth Thomason, Jean Smart, Dixie Carter, Annie Potts, Delta Burke.

CHAPTER ONE

One Woman's Design

QUOTE

"Our goal on *Designing Women* was to be funny, to present a winning portrayal of Southerners, and to show beautiful feminists who were man loving, politically incorrect, and able to poke fun at themselves. The cast was deadly brilliant and we were given complete artistic freedom. It was sublime."

—Linda Bloodworth Thomason,
series creator

DESIGNING WOMEN WAS THE GIFT of one woman, Linda Bloodworth Thomason. Linda was born in Poplar Bluff, Missouri, where her family moved after her grandfather, an Arkansas attorney who represented blacks and welcomed them into his home, was shot and wounded by the Ku Klux Klan.

Growing up a little like Scout in *To Kill a Mockingbird*, Linda loved her birthplace so much she made it the hometown of Charlene Frazier. Linda says in her family, you were sent to your room if you didn't have an opinion, teaching her early on never to be without a well thought out assessment for any subject that might come up. Linda's father, Ralph Bloodworth Sr., was a lawyer who practiced with his brothers, Howard and Charles. Charles was one of the Nuremberg war crimes prosecutors. Howard flew his own plane, was friendly with Elvis, and portrayed Charlene's uncle in the wedding episode, "Come On and Marry Me, Bill," where he gave the wedding toast. After years of listening to these men's passionate discussions of literature, politics, and religion, Linda has often been quoted as saying she created the Designing Women by giving the men in her family sex change operations.

Linda obtained a bachelor of arts degree in English from the University of Missouri at Columbia. After graduation, she moved to Los Angeles, where she taught English at Jordan High School, located in the racially charged Watts district.

It was about this time Linda began writing with Mary Kay Place. Together, they wrote for *Rhoda*, *One Day at a Time*, and *M*A*S*H*, where their first episode was nominated for an Emmy. Linda and Mary Kay's influence on *M*A*S*H* is largely credited with the evolution of Loretta Swit's character from tyrannical head nurse to a more humane member of the hospital staff. In their first episode, "Hot Lips and Empty Arms," Margaret ends her dysfunctional relationship with Major Frank Burns. (Totally Useless Trivia: "Hot Lips and Empty Arms" also included the first appearance of Kellye Nakahara, who would be seen in fifty-five *M*A*S*H* episodes as bubbly, Hawaiian Nurse Kellye.) For the fifth season, Linda and Mary Kay contributed an episode called "The Nurses," which includes a gut-wrenching speech in which Margaret lambastes the nurses for excluding her from their friendships and social activities. It was the kind of amusing, heartfelt speech that would become the benchmark of so many of *Designing Women*'s finest moments.

A few years later Linda Bloodworth met Harry Thomason on the Columbia Studio lot. They were surprised to discover that the show he was producing for ABC, *The Fall Guy*, was scheduled opposite *Filthy Rich*, Linda's spoof of nighttime soap operas. Harry says, "Our shows went against each other and mine killed hers, so she married the competition." In July of 1983, Linda and Harry were married in Poplar Bluff. They formed Mozark Productions later that same year. The name is a tribute to both their home states, Missouri and Arkansas.

Filthy Rich may not have been a huge ratings success, but it introduced Linda to Dixie Carter and Delta Burke. Later in 1985, while working with husband Harry Thomason on the short-lived series, *Lime Street*, Linda met

Annie Potts and Jean Smart, who played international jewel-thieving sisters in one episode.

Ordinarily, when a writer has an idea for a new situation comedy, a good deal of descriptive information about the potential series is required. Usually, there are pages of background on the show's main characters, an outline for a pilot episode, and ten or twelve ideas for future episodes. All this information is discussed with network executives and hopefully, the network will ask for a pilot script to be written. When Linda Bloodworth Thomason pitched her new series to CBS, she only knew that she wanted to write for four voices—Delta Burke,

A BRIEF HISTORY OF TIMESLOT

During the course of a seven season run, *Designing Women* went through nine schedule changes.

September 1986–November 1986: Monday at 9:30
December 1986–January 1987: Thursday at 9:30
February 1987: Sunday at 9:00
March 1987–February 1988: Monday at 9:30
February 1988–June 1988: Monday at 8:30
June 1988–September 1989: Monday at 9:30
September 1989–October 1989: Monday at 10:00
November 1989–September 1992: Monday 9:30
September 1992–May 1993: Friday 9:00

Dixie Carter, Annie Potts, and Jean Smart—and *Designing Women* was born.

There was one small glitch. Network executives were concerned about repeating the Burke/Carter duo from *Filthy Rich*. They approved Annie Potts, Jean Smart, and Dixie Carter, but insisted that Linda use a different actress for the fourth role. CBS wanted Lorna Patterson, who had starred in their *Private Benjamin* series, for the part of Suzanne. A great actress, Patterson simply wasn't right for the role—especially when all the parts had been tailor-made for specific actresses. After a week of rehearsal, the night before the pilot was to go before the cameras, Linda made a plea to CBS network officials, letting them know how crucial she felt it was to have Delta Burke portray Suzanne Sugarbaker. The network relented and Linda surprised the other actresses by bringing Delta Burke to the soundstage.

Julia and Suzanne with Noel the pig from the episode
"I'll Be Home for Christmas."

CHAPTER TWO

Meet the Designing Women (Plus One Ex-Con and a Little Fruitcake)

QUOTE

[on . . . JULIA SUGAR-BAKER (Dixie Carter)]

"A woman who ran a perpetual temperature from hot porcelain to cool steel and could fan a fire with a quick sashay of her walk."

—Dash Goff, the writer

JULIA SUGARBAKER WAS A BOLD, independent, self-confident, sassy, no-nonsense Southern lady. Her passionate beliefs and rapid-fire speeches earned her the nickname "The Terminator." Dash Goff, Suzanne's writer ex-husband, believed Julia belonged to "a time before flirting became extinct, when letter writing was an art, stationery was engraved, and dinner was an event."

Julia's mother, Perky (Louise Latham), was married five times, twice to Julia's father. Julia was born during her parents' first marriage. A few years later, Mr. Sugarbaker had a brief dalliance with a Radio City Music Hall Rockette named Dee Dee, who became pregnant. Mr. Sugarbaker divorced Perky and married Dee Dee, at least long enough for half brother, Clayton Sugarbaker, to have a legitimate birth. Shortly after, Mr. Sugarbaker divorced Dee Dee the Rockette, remarried Perky, and Suzanne was born. During the first season, Perky visited for Thanksgiving, with Bernice Clifton in tow. Soon after, Perky moved to Japan and was never seen on the show again.

Donald Gilman (Ray Buktenica), a high school chum of Julia, remembered her as a cross between Jennifer Jones and Veronica from the Archie comics. He recalled how she would roar onto the high school campus in her grandfather's Aston Martin and was the only person in their speech class to support Hubert Humphrey. Always the rebel, Julia attended Chapel Hill University where she was kicked out of the Tri-Delt sorority for refusing to wear a girdle on campus. She marched for civil rights in Selma, Alabama, and was arrested for protesting so many times according to Suzanne it almost turned their mother's hair white.

It was not easy for Julia to recover from the loss of her husband, Hayden McIlroy, who died after suffering several heart attacks. In the year following Hayden's death, Julia formed the Sugarbaker design firm and spent her free time painting and avoiding life in general. This might have continued for years, if not for dramatic barrister, Reese Watson (Hal Holbrook). The first thing Reese did was honestly tell Julia how much he hated her paintings. A widower, Reese was able to show Julia that loving each other did not mean they had to love their former spouses any less, an important lesson that Julia is later able to share with

THE BIG KIMONO

In the course of the series, several characters were said to have moved to Japan. This was known among the production staff as getting "The Big Kimono." In season one, Julia and Suzanne's mother threatened to move to Montana, but ultimately ended up in Japan. Later during the same season, when Charlene became seriously involved with boyfriend Mason Dodd, he, too, was sent to live in the Far East.

Finally, when Delta Burke left the show after season five, we were told that Suzanne had moved to Japan to be closer to their mother. Julia had this to say of Suzanne's move: "She was attracted to the Japanese economy. They have a large elderly population and Suzanne has dated most of the men in this country."

Charlene's Bill. Julia and Reese enjoyed a volatile but fulfilling relationship until he also died of a sudden coronary. Julia and Hayden had only one child, a son, Payne (George Newburn). During the series, Payne graduates from college, marries his college sweetheart, Sylvie, and moves to New York to begin a career in publishing.

QUOTE

[on . . . SUZANNE SUGAR-BAKER (Delta Burke)]

"She had one of those guilty smiles, where the corners of the mouth turned upward, just in time to keep the lips quiet, leaving a man to wonder if she'd wrecked his car, slept with his best friend, or given all his clothes to the Salvation Army."

—Dash Goff, the writer

Suzanne believed that beauty was the key to success in life. Perky predicted, quite accurately, that Suzanne would grow up to be the center of attention. It is this desire for the spotlight that led her to the beauty pageant circles. Suzanne won eleven beauty titles ranging from Miss Georgia World to Miss Atlanta Arboretum and prided herself on having a pageant story for any occasion.

Suzanne constantly dated elderly, extremely wealthy men, constantly complaining about intrusive nurses, unwieldy oxygen tanks, dates canceling because of broken hips, and stints in ICU. Suzanne may have dated the elderly, but she married the young and virile, three times. The great love of Suzanne's life was Dash Goff (Gerald McRaney), a Southern writer who occasionally returned to Suzanne for inspiration. They met when Suzanne was selling kisses at the Pi Phi booth at her university, Ol' Miss. According to Dash, she had the highest prices and the longest lines. Dash also had the distinct honor of being the only poor person Suzanne ever kissed. Their marriage was always rocky, possibly the roughest patch being when Suzanne carelessly threw out Dash's third novel with the trash.

Her second husband, Jack Dent (Gregg Henry), played baseball for the Atlanta Braves. Husband number three was Jay Benton Stonecipher. Very little is known about this marriage. Julia likes to point out that the turban Suzanne wore for the wedding was a severe fashion mistake. Suzanne, herself, believed the main problem with this marriage was that Jay Benton had never dated anyone else and, therefore, had no stories for her about how other women fell short. Suzanne claimed that all her ex-husbands had tried to reconcile with her, but it never worked. "They make promises for the first few weeks. They'll say stuff like, 'Okay, we'll never try to get into your bathroom again,' or 'We'll never make love to you on the days you've just had your hair done,' or 'We'll never ask you to get in any position other than the normal sleeping one, lying flat on your back, head on pillow,' but it doesn't last."

Suzanne could be thoughtless and self-centered. She was known to stretch out on top of people on airplanes, or at the very least, rest her pocketbook on top of some unsuspecting passenger. Over the years, many women were resentful of Suzanne because of the attention she received from their husbands and boyfriends. Suzanne usually overcompensated for this by assuming that all women in the world were jealous of her. Deep down, Suzanne was actually hurt by her lack of female friend-ships and was envious of the close relationship shared by Charlene and Mary Jo. Oddly enough, Suzanne was most vulnerable and honest with Anthony, treating him as a surrogate best girlfriend. Despite her endless refer-ences to his unfortunate incarceration, Suzanne and Anthony shared a bond that the other women found baffling. Suzanne actually admitted to Anthony that other women treated her as if she had no feelings. She also shared her philosophy that life is much easier if you don't get too involved. If you wait until things are forced on you, she surmised, you can never be blamed for any-thing. And if a situation got too sticky, Suzanne had an alias at her fingertips. In the spirit of Phoebe Buffet's Regina Phalange and Karen Walker's Anastasia Beaverhausen, at the first sign of trouble, Suzanne always claimed to be Helen Van Patterson Patton, a woman who once tried to have her blackballed on the beauty pageant judge circuit.

Suzanne's deepest fear may have been that her beauty was her only asset. She admitted to Julia that winning her crowns was the greatest part of her life and she was afraid that nothing else would ever equal that. Julia was quick to criticize Suzanne, but even quicker to defend her. When Mary Jo and Charlene accused Suzanne of being too shallow to date a fantastic man because of his blindness, Julia explained that the situation played on all of Suzanne's insecurities. Her reliance on her beauty, her walk, and her flirtatious glances would never work on a blind man and Suzanne was afraid that her inner self wasn't good enough.

Suzanne's selfishness seemed to fall away during a crisis. When Bill was sent to the Persian Gulf, she told Charlene she'd be happy to call the Air Force and inform them Bill is a homosexual. She handled everything for Julia when Reese had his first heart attack and took over again when he died unexpectedly. She became a foster mother for an Asian orphan, Li Sing (Connie Lew)—making over the little girl as a miniature version of herself. Li Sing was a sponge for Suzanne's version of etiquette, telling everyone that a linen hankie is a sign of good breeding and bad manners were worse than having no money. Suzanne had a great deal of love to give and for several years, lavished it on a pet pig named Noel. A

Christmas gift from Consuela's meat packing family, Suzanne spent many happy afternoons driving Noel around Atlanta in her convertible with the top down, making frequent stops at the Dairy Queen for Buster

THIS LITTLE PIGGY

Noel the pig made her debut on the season two holiday episode, "I'll Be Home for Christmas." Series Costume Designer Cliff Chally recalled designing a dress for Noel in lavender to match the dress Suzanne was wearing. Then came the issue of who would actually construct the garment. Seamstresses on the studio lot said it was not their job because they did not sew clothing that was to be worn by an animal. Tailors said it was not their job because it was a dress and they only made clothing for men. To this day no one will admit who made the pig's dress, but finally the outfit was sewn and it came time to get the pig into it.

Cliff, who is famous for his dapper appearance, always in jacket and tie, described finding himself outside the soundstage on hands and knees trying to wrestle a pig into a dress. "The animal trainer was helping. The pig was squealing and resisting. An old grip, who was standing nearby smoking and watching, finally remarked, 'I don't think she likes the color.'"

Ultimately, Cliff prevailed. Noel made her debut in a lavender gown and Cliff spent the rest of the night with a pig's hoofprints all over his necktie.

Bars. After the pig ran away, Suzanne was always on the lookout for outlets for her nurturing side, and everyone from Charlene's new baby to Anthony was fair game.

A proud member of the National Rifle Association, Suzanne was fascinated with weapons. She purchased a large semi-automatic rifle, but traded down to a small handgun after accidentally firing it at Julia, Mary Jo, and Charlene. She was also forced to bankroll a black history reading room at Anthony's college after she accidentally shot him, mistaking him for a prowler.

According to Suzanne Sugarbaker

Pigs are preferable to children, but if you do find yourself stuck with a kid, here's what Suzanne would do. "Once they're housebroken, they go straight off to military school and then, if they make good grades, they can come home when they're twenty-one—providing they don't play their stereo too loud."

QUOTE

[on . . . MARY JO SHIVELY (Annie Potts)]

"Mary Jo is part calico choir girl and part satin dancehall doll. With amber eyes and a dash of hellcat red in her hair. The kind of woman a man wants in his bedroom when he's sick, and in his bed when he's not."

—Dash Goff, the writer

Mary Jo Shively was a devoted mother, a meticulous worker, a loyal friend, and probably the character who changed the most over the course of the series. During the first season, Mary Jo was extremely shy and easily intimidated, but her divorce forced her to discover and call forth her own inner strength. Mary Jo was as passionate about her convictions as Julia, but had much greater difficulty expressing her beliefs to others. By season seven, she had studied under "The Terminator" and could easily give Julia a run for her money.

Mary Jo grew up in Franklin, Kentucky, praying for snow days. Her father, Davis Jackson (Geoffrey Lewis), a veterinarian, and her mother, Darla (Jackie Joseph), a housewife, were divorced and even though Mary Jo was a divorced parent herself, she had a difficult time accepting her parent's split. She had an older brother, Skip (Blake Clark), who made her life miserable by calling her Mary Joseph and treating her like the brother he would have preferred, and a sister, Patty.

In college, Mary Jo minored in French art. She and Ted Shively (Scott Bakula), her ex-husband, grew up together and married very young. Other than an opal pinkie ring, Ted Shively was never any good at giving gifts. Instead of an engagement ring, Ted presented Mary Jo with a gift certificate, and every year on her birthday she received a card saying a donation had been made in her name to the United Way. Due to poor undergraduate grades, Ted was only accepted to a medical school in Guadalajara. They moved there when Mary Jo was six months pregnant with their first child, Claudia Marie (Priscilla Weems). Mary Jo financed Ted's medical education by working as a file clerk during the day and waiting tables at night. In between jobs, Mary Jo honed her bargaining skills when, after a week of paying whatever price street vendors named, Mary Jo thought Guadalajara was going to be too expensive a place for them to live. When Ted graduated, they returned to the States and he opened his gynecological practice. It was during this time that the couple occupied an apartment next door to Charlene Frazier and the two ladies formed their close friendship. Although it was Mary Jo who actually filed for divorce, Ted let her know he wanted it in a hundred little ways—he had a hundred little girlfriends. Their second child, Quinton (Brian Lando), had been born by this time. Mary Jo sued for child support only. When Julia expresses her shock that Mary Jo didn't ask for alimony, Mary Jo admitted she had her heart set on the death penalty.

It took a great deal of courage for Mary Jo to go out on her first date after her divorce. Suzanne set her up with J. D. Shackleford (Richard Gilliland), a talent scout for the Atlanta Braves. J. D. was also recently divorced with three children. The direct opposite of Ted, he and Mary Jo developed a mutually supportive relationship that lasted several years. They eventually reached a point where it was time to either marry or break up. They decided to split up, but still remained close friends.

After J. D., Mary Jo didn't seem to have much luck in the romance department. She briefly dated Julia's minister, Gene Chapman (Bruce Davison). Attempting to "date like a man," led her to unsuccessful dates with Kenny Rayburn (William Bell Sullivan), a frat boy type in his late twenties, and Craig Holman (Patrick Warburton), a dumb but well muscled himbo. Mary Jo met Craig when he was "casual dad" in the Americana suite of the Home Expo. She was ultimately forced to admit he was "dumber than a box of rocks."

By the end of the series, Mary Jo was feeling the urge to become a mother again and was attempting to become pregnant through artificial insemination.

QUOTE

[on . . . CHARLENE FRAZIER (Jean Smart)]

"Charlene, she was all cotton candy and pink lemonade, with legs that stretch out for five or six miles and one of those laughs that make you feel like ridin' around in a convertible."

—Dash Goff, the writer

Charlene Frazier was raised a strict Southern Baptist in the small town of Poplar Bluff, Missouri. She was the eldest of thirteen children born to Norvelle "Bud" Frazier (James Ray and Barry Corbin) and Ione "Dot" Hogg (Ronnie Claire Edwards). Her sisters were Carlene, Harlene, Marlene, Darlene, and the deceased Pat, whom she mentions when speaking to Dolly Parton, her guardian movie star. Charlene's brothers were Dwayne, Frank, Virgil, Robert, Odell, Billy Hugh, and the baby of the family, Harold Thomas. Things always happened to Charlene. She had been in nine car accidents, had a pet struck by lightning, and was once hijacked on the way to Furniture Mart. Her naive and trusting personality could be as obnoxious as it was endearing.

Charlene never met a stranger and could find the good in anyone. Her mother said the family had more dinners with Jehovah's Witnesses, Avon ladies, and Fuller Brush men than anyone in their area, at little Charlene's invitation. Mary Jo remarked that Charlene was the kind of woman "who would have dated Lee Harvey Oswald in high school." Charlene and Mary Jo shared a very special bond, but even Mary Jo could get frustrated by what that great sage, Julia Sugarbaker, referred to as Charlene's "unequaled ability to be fascinated at absolutely nothing." Charlene's "thirst for knowledge" equipped her with comments and insights gleaned from her exploration of everything from *National Geographic* to the *National Enquirer*. She was also very proud of her knowledge of all the world's capitals.

At an early age, Charlene dreamed of becoming a preacher and traveling the world spreading the word of God. She also had fantasies of becoming a country music singer and fulfilling her mother's fantasy of singing at the Grand Ole Opry. During high school, Charlene worked as a carhop at A&W and an usherette at the Rodgers Theatre. She attended the Three Rivers Secretarial Academy and then moved to Little Rock, Arkansas, where she became a secretary at the state capitol. From there, she moved to Atlanta where she was a secretary for Hayden McIlroy, Julia's husband, until his death. When Julia decided to form Sugarbaker's design firm, she asked Charlene to be the office manager and an equal partner. While the business was getting started, Charlene sold cosmetics on the side and eventually got her real estate agent's license.

Though constantly guided by her psychic advisor, Tovah of Biloxi, the Charlene we met at the beginning of the series was famous for attracting all the wrong men. High school friend, Monette, claimed Charlene was voted Most Likely to Date a Convict. From her high school prom date who didn't wear a shirt under his tux jacket to a bank robber, Suzanne claimed Charlene had been involved with "every stray dog in the western world." Her gullible nature combined with her gorgeous looks to make her an easy target for con men. The other women were convinced that Shadow (Thomas Callaway), a man with a bullet hole in his pants, was another bad choice. They were shocked when his claim of being a secret government agent doing undercover work in jail proved to be on the level.

Charlene's search for the right man ended when Colonel Bill Stillfield arrived on the scene. Charlene had recently told her friends she wanted a soldier for her birthday. Theirs was a whirlwind romance, culminating in a huge church wedding and the birth of their first child, Olivia Frazier Stillfield, nine months later. Like Elvis and Priscilla, Charlene and Bill got pregnant on their honeymoon. When Bill was stationed in England, Charlene's sister, Carlene Dobber, arrived to take over as office manager.

According to Suzanne Sugarbaker
There was a patron saint for homosexuals called Saint Francis of a Sissy.

Anthony Bouvier (Meshach Taylor)

The token male of the series, deliveryman Anthony Bouvier, was originally to be a minor recurring character. However, his chemistry with the women proved to be too hard to resist. Halfway through the premier season, it became clear Anthony was destined to be a permanent member of the family.

Abandoned when he was two weeks old by his drug-addicted mother, Anthony did not have an easy start in the world. He was raised by his strict but loving grandmother, a schoolteacher he calls Dondi (Frances E. Williams and Beah Richards). Anthony met his father when Charlene convinced the women to hire a private investigator to track the man down as a gift for Anthony's thirtieth birthday. His name was Charles Clarence Monroe (Bill Cobbs) and he lived in New Orleans. At first, Anthony was not too pleased by the reunion, but finally decided to get to know his dad. Anthony had brothers and sisters scattered all over the country. One brother, Delman, performed on stage with Anthony when they were very young. They were billed as the Twin Little Richards. Anthony also mentioned his Uncle Willie, who, when money was too scarce for the family to afford Christmas presents, told little Anthony terrible stories of the deaths of Santa and his elves.

As a teenager, Anthony worked as a busboy at the exclusive Beaumont Driving Club. He would have graduated from high school in 1977, but was arrested for his involvement in a convenience store robbery. Anthony was waiting in the car while his friends went in to buy beer. Without his knowledge, they decided to take the contents of the cash register instead. As a result, Anthony spent time in jail, a period he refers to as his "unfortunate incarceration." He often regaled the ladies with dark stories of his prison days, including tales of his cellmate, T. Tommy Reed (M. C. Gainey), a man who checked out a book on etiquette from the prison library and then stabbed a fellow prisoner for serving him from the wrong side. T. Tommy had a special fondness for Anthony, often forcing him to dance, and once, when he was briefly out of prison, expecting Anthony to become his business partner.

After starting work at Sugarbaker's, Anthony did many things to improve his life, in spite of the fact that Suzanne continued to turn his name in to the authorities every time there was a police composite of a black man on the evening news. He graduated from Kennesaw Junior College, got his contracting license, and moved on to law school. Wanting to give back as much as he could, Anthony became involved with a citizen's rights coalition, the Big Brothers program, and received the Bootstrap Award from the governor of Georgia.

Over the course of the series, Anthony developed a bond with Suzanne that the other women found extremely confusing. He seemed to be her "best girlfriend," running errands, chauffeuring her pet pig, and even waxing her legs when Conseula got the wax too hot and burned her.

According to Meshach Taylor, "A lot of people still think Anthony is gay . . . He always had girlfriends and always was a gentleman with the ladies. And I think that a lot of people have felt and some people have said to me, if he wasn't gay, why wasn't he trying to get at all those girls? And that kind of begs the question, if you work with women are you supposed to try to have sex with them all the time? Can you just have friendship that is based on the fact that you have mutual respect and have a business mind about the things you're doing?"

Obviously, Anthony was not gay. Over the course of the series he had quite a few girlfriends. Once he got his life in order, he became involved with Lita Ford (Mariann Aalda), a super yuppie who wanted to make Anthony into the black Donald Trump. The ladies, especially Suzanne, despised her. Later he started a relationship with his crazy New Year's Eve blind date, Vanessa Hargraves (Olivia Brown). Vanessa, however, disappeared from the show during season five. Season six ended with a cliff-hanger: Anthony's announcement of his engagement to the ultra-rich Vanessa Chamberlain (Jackee Harry), a woman who seemed intent on taking over the business herself.

A few episodes into season seven, Vanessa Chamberlain dumped Anthony. The ladies dragged him to Las Vegas in an attempt to break his depression and he ended up marrying showgirl Etienne Toussaint (Sheryl Lee Ralph), during a drunken binge.

According to Suzanne Sugarbaker

Sex is way overrated. "I have never understood why everybody gets so crazy over sex anyway. I mean, when you think about it, it's pretty silly. And it's silly lookin', too. And it messes up your hair. I don't think it's something we would've ever come up with on our own . . . It just has to be hormones. Otherwise, no rational person would be runnin' around trying to link up with other people in that way. When you get right down to it, it's just an odd thing to do. I mean, it's okay, but we're talking about what? Six or seven seconds here? It's sure not as good as say, having somebody put a crown on your head or shopping."

Bernice Clifton (Alice Ghostley), "The Little Fruitcake"

The most frequent guest star of the series, Alice Ghostley, appeared as Bernice Clifton in forty-six episodes over the course of seven seasons. Believe it or not, Ms. Ghostley was not the first person considered for the role. Series Casting Director Fran Bascom remembered Dody Goodman, famous for *Mary Hartman, Mary Hartman* and *Grease*, who was approached, but didn't want to play such a daffy character. Lucky for us, Alice Ghostley had no such qualms. Her episodes outnumbered those of later series regulars Allison, B. J., and Carlene. In the final season, Bernice appeared in almost every episode.

Bernice Clifton was the addled best friend of Suzanne and Julia's mother, Perky. After Perky moved to Japan, the ladies looked after Mrs. Clifton at Perky's request. Keeping up with Bernice could be extremely difficult since she had an arterial flow problem above the neck that caused her to behave shockingly. Bernice sent the women health tips, entered them in contests, and, during her Mrs. Senior Citizen Pageant, referred to them as her daughters. Bernice lived in a retirement community called Hillcrest Leisure Land.

Bernice's late husband, Louis Clifton, came from a circus family where he was billed as "The Dancing Fool." One of Louis' uncles was a fire-eater, a talent he taught to Bernice. She had a charm-free niece named Phyllis McGuire (Leslie Ackerman) and twin great-nephews, Nick and Dick, though Bernice thought both boys were named Dick. Her father was a Southern Baptist minister and when "all her circuits were burning," Bernice was a scripture expert.

Bernice's odd behavior drove Suzanne absolutely crazy and she often referred to Bernice as a "little fruit-cake." Bernice had a very special relationship with Anthony, whom she often claimed was her illegitimate son. She just as frequently accused Anthony of being attracted to her and jealously referred to his various girlfriends as she-beasts. During season six, Bernice's arterial flow seemed to be down to a trickle and she developed the habit of singing "Black Man, Black Man," whenever Anthony was within earshot.

Bernice was very active, but she was known to loudly question the concept that growing old gives you a talent for arts and crafts. Her one attempt at pottery produced nothing but a couple of gladiator breastplates. Bernice's ability to drive was one of the series inconsistencies. In season one, she claimed to have taught herself, but later Anthony ends up spending many afternoons shuttling Bernice around town.

According to Suzanne Sugarbaker

With Julia as his overbearing mother it is almost a miracle that Payne didn't turn out to be gay. Especially since Payne is a homosexual name. Other homosexual names are Darrel, Wade, Tommy, Peter, and Dennis. Heterosexual names are Chester and Ralph.

Julia: "No, thank you. I'll feel them some other time."
Mary Jo is thrilled to show off her potential new breast.

CHAPTER THREE

Season One, 1986-1987

DESIGNING WOMEN DEBUTED on September 29, 1986—introducing the four ladies who provided the humor for the first five years. Together, they ran a newly formed interior design business, Sugarbakers and Associates, in Atlanta, Georgia. One of the few sitcoms of its time that didn't talk down to viewers, Linda Bloodworth Thomason's show was filled with sharp dialogue and the four women had an amazing chemistry.

Designing Women earned an immediate following and good enough ratings in its Monday night 9:30 time slot for CBS to decide to try it against Thursday night's heavy hitters. Landing on Thursday night at 9:00 P.M., the series was up against *Cheers* and *Night Court* on NBC and *Dynasty* spin-off *The Colbys* on ABC. Needless to say, the freshman series' ratings failed to bring down the competition. Again, the network decided to adjust time slots. This time *Designing Women* was moved to Sunday night at 9:00, competing with various Sunday night movies. Again, the ratings failed to measure up. At this point, CBS placed a show it had considered a hit on indefinite hiatus.

Indefinite hiatus is polite terminology for the fast track to cancellation.

Fortunately, a fledgling media group called Viewers for Quality Television was not ready to give up the series. They organized the fans, petitioned advertisers, and wrote over 50,000 letters to CBS. Finally relenting, CBS Entertainment President Bud Grant sent a limo to drive the four stars of *Designing Women* to CBS so they could witness as he ceremoniously raised a white surrender flag and put the series back on the schedule in its original, successful Monday night time period. Back where it belonged, the series grew into a top twenty hit.

During the first season, Linda Bloodworth Thomason wrote episodes dealing with such serious issues as sexual harassment and breast cancer. The hour-long episode "Old Spouses Never Die," which dealt with Charlene's breast cancer scare, was dedicated to Harry Thomason's mother, Pauline, who died of breast cancer.

Suzanne's interest in sex is much more direct in season one, causing Julia to comment, if sex were fast food, Suzanne would have an arch over her bed. Julia also told Mary Jo and Charlene that when she and Suzanne were dating boys, their mother always gave them a dime to call home in case a date got too fresh. Suzanne eventually used her dimes to tour Europe. Starting in the pilot, when she dated Mary Jo's ex-husband Ted, and continuing through encounters with her own ex-husband Jack Dent, in the first season Suzanne was not the one who dated men who worried about broken hips.

Julia was every bit the big-shouldered broad in season one, dealing with a young, female barracuda lawyer who set her sights on stealing Reese and a forty-year-old college professor who wanted to do the same thing to her son, Payne.

Recently divorced, Mary Jo was thrown back into the world of dating when Suzanne fixed her up with Atlanta Braves baseball recruiter, J. D. Shackleford. In this first season, it was Mary Jo who had the great affection for slumber parties that will later become a major trait of Charlene.

Charlene's entire family from Poplar Bluff visited just in time to witness her being fleeced by con man Gaylon King (Michael Ross), who promised to make her a big country music star. Charlene was kept very busy in the romance department during season one, dating secret government agent Shadow, three-hundred-pound entrepreneur Mason Dodd, and married man Ed Boeving. Finally, Charlene was floored to find out that fellow high school cheerleader Monette Marlin (Bobbie Faye Ferguson) had become a madam, responding in typical Charlene fashion to the news that Monette was practicing the world's oldest profession with, "Monette's a carpenter?"

In another favorite episode of the first season, Suzanne's maid, Consuela, put a voodoo curse on her. Yet another of Charlene's boyfriends got the women arrested when the incredibly cheap furniture he sold them turned out to be stolen. The Thanksgiving episode included the only appearance of Perky Sugarbaker (Louise Latham), Julia and Suzanne's mother. In the episode, the ladies suspected Anthony of murdering a client.

SEASON ONE
FAVORITE QUOTES

From "Bachelor Suite" by Linda Bloodworth Thomason.

JULIA: I keep a list of people who have touched my behind without permission. Some of them have died unnatural and untimely deaths.

From "Seams from a Marriage" by E. Jack Kaplan.

SUZANNE: What I don't understand is why you always hear about men changing into women and you almost never hear about women changing into men.
JULIA: My guess is it would be too hard to find a donor.

From "Nashville Bound" by Linda Bloodworth Thomason.

MARY JO: I mean, Charlene is one of those women that you read about in the *National Enquirer*. You know, the ones who don't know they're pregnant. And one day they're just sittin' around, sippin' on a soda and all of a sudden, they look down and say, "My stars! Would you look at this! I just had a baby!" That's Charlene.

Season One Episodes

Pilot
Written by Linda Bloodworth Thomason
Directed by Ellen Falcon
Suzanne dates Mary Jo's ex-husband.

The Beauty Contest
Written by Linda Bloodworth Thomason
Directed by Jack Shea
Charlene enters Mary Jo's daughter in Miss
    Pre-Teen Atlanta.

A Big Affair
Written by Linda Bloodworth Thomason
Directed by Jack Shea
Charlene dates 320-pound entrepreneur,
    Mason Dodd.

Julia's Son
Written by Linda Bloodworth Thomason
Directed by Jack Shea
Payne brings home his first serious girlfriend, who is
    twenty years his senior.

Mary Jo's First Date
Written by Cheryl Gard
Directed by Jack Shea

Suzanne fixes Mary Jo up with J. D. Shackleford, a
talent scout for the Atlanta Braves.

Design House
Written by Joan Brooker and Nancy Eddo
Directed by Jack Shea
Suzanne's first attempt at decorating goes up
in smoke.

Perky's Visit
Written by Linda Bloodworth Thomason
Directed by Jack Shea
Julia and Suzanne's mother visits for Thanksgiving
with Bernice Clifton in tow.

I Do, I Don't
Written by Emily Marshall
Directed by Jack Shea
Julia and Reese drink too much champagne
and elope.

The IT Men
Written by Emily Marshall
Directed by Jack Shea
Charlene is dating a married man.

The Slumber Party
Written by Linda Bloodworth Thomason
Directed by Jack Shea
Suzanne's maid, Consuela, puts a voodoo curse
on her.

New Year's Daze
Written by Trish Vradenburg
Directed by David Steinberg
Charlene's date for New Year's Eve has just
    escaped from jail.

Old Spouses Never Die (hour-long episode)
Written by Linda Bloodworth Thomason
Directed by Barnet Kellman
Charlene finds a lump in her breast. Mary Jo and
    J. D. move their relationship into the bedroom.

Monette
Written by Linda Bloodworth Thomason
Directed by Barnet Kellman
Charlene's old friend from high school is a madam.

And Justice for Paul
Written by Trish Vradenberg
Directed by Jack Shea
The ladies end up in jail when they buy bargain
    furniture that turns out to be stolen.

Reese's Friend
Written by Linda Bloodworth Thomason
Directed by Arlene Sanford
Julia is jealous of a young lawyer who is
    after Reese.

Nashville Bound
Written by Linda Bloodworth Thomason

Directed by Harry Thomason
Charlene is conned out of several thousand dollars by a
  manager who claims he can make her a country
  music singing star.

Oh, Suzannah
Written by Linda Bloodworth Thomason
Directed by Matthew Diamond
Suzanne becomes a foster mother for a month.

Mary Jo's Dad Dates Charlene
Written by Linda Bloodworth Thomason
Directed by Jack Shea
Charlene and Mary Jo's father hit it off when he comes
  for a visit.

Seams from a Marriage
Written by E. Jack Kaplan
Directed by Jack Shea
Superwealthy clients make the design firm miserable
  with their demands.

Grand Slam, Thank You, Ma'am
Written by Linda Bloodworth Thomason
Directed by Barnet Kellman
Suzanne's ex-husband, baseball player Jack Dent, writes
  a book about his experiences with groupies while he
  was married to her.

Bachelor Suite
Written by Linda Bloodworth Thomason

Directed by Jack Shea
A client sexually harasses Mary Jo.

According to Suzanne Sugarbaker

Travel and cultural experiences in general are to be avoided. Suzanne made it clear she had no intention of trudging through one more art museum filled with paintings of small-busted women with large butts lying around naked outdoors, eating fruit. As for seeing the "real" side of any country, Suzanne had this to say: "I have noticed that whenever people talk about seeing the real anything, what they're talking about is basically hanging around with poor people! I say, I don't hang around with poor people at home . . . why should I do it on my vacation?"

Bernice (Alice Ghostley) joins Suzanne, Julia, and Mary Jo in serenading Charlene at her bachelorette slumber party in "Come On and Marry Me, Bill."

CHAPTER FOUR

Season Two, 1987–1988

SEASON TWO DELIVERED much more consistent characters, due in no small way to the fact that Linda Bloodworth Thomason wrote every episode of the season by herself. There was no writing staff and Linda did an astounding job of tailoring each character to each actor's particular strength.

Suzanne's first husband, the writer Dash Goff (Gerald McRaney), makes his first appearance when his latest novel, *Being Belled*, is poorly received and he turns to Suzanne for inspiration. This was Delta's introduction to Gerald McRaney, the man she would later marry. It was in this season that Suzanne's accountant, Reggie Mac Dawson (Danny Thomason) absconded with her entire life savings, causing her to almost marry an eighty-year-old man for his money, sell Naughty Lady Lingerie, and move in with Charlene. Finally, Suzanne took all the cash she could scrape together to Atlantic City, where, armed with Consuela's good luck chant, she managed to gamble her way back to her wealthier lifestyle. In this season, Suzanne almost got into the Beaumont Driving Club—a very exclusive club she considered the pinnacle of Atlanta high society.

Julia had two especially unforgettable episodes in season two. One centered on her relationship with Reese Watson. When Reese suffered a heart attack, we found out more about the death of Julia's husband, Hayden McIlroy. We were also treated to a peek at the real-life chemistry between Dixie Carter and her husband, Hal Holbrook, which jumped off the screen when Julia showed up at Reese's home in the middle of the afternoon wearing nothing but a trench coat over her negligee. The other brilliant moment for Julia was an episode Dixie Carter claims as one of her personal favorites, "How Great Thou Art." In it, Julia was selected to sing the hymn at the closing ceremony of a huge church conference. At first afraid she would not be able to hit the high notes, she refused, but ultimately she was inspired to sing by Charlene's own crisis of faith.

We learned a great deal more of Anthony's history in this season, finding out that he had been wrongly convicted. His off-the-wall friendship with Suzanne was solidified when the two of them were forced to spend the night together in a cheap motel during a blizzard.

Charlene's weekly visits to her psychic, Tovah of Biloxi, continued, but her life was forever altered by the introduction of Doug Barr in the role of Colonel Bill Stillfield. Charlene's main story lines of this year focused on the ups and downs of their growing relationship, complete with a fantastic World War II dream sequence that included Mary Jo as a brassy, sassy cigarette girl,

Suzanne as the baton-twirling, gasoline-siphoning Miss War Bonds, and Julia in the role of a singing air raid warden, who was called upon to tell off Hitler.

Alice Ghostley, who was seen only once during the first season, was back several times as widow Bernice Clifton. She competed in a Mrs. Senior Citizen Beauty Contest and needed Suzanne to be her coach. Bernice also attempted to help Mary Jo prepare for her debate in "Killing All the Right People" by giving her own views on safe sex.

YOU'VE BEEN TERMINATED . . .

From the battle of the sexes in "Reservations for Eight."

JULIA: In general, it has been the men who have done the raping and the robbing and the killing and the warmongering for the last two thousand years. And it's been the men who have done the pillaging and the beheading and the subjugating of whole races into slavery. It has been the men who have done the lawmaking and the moneymaking and the most of the mischief making! So if the world isn't quite what you had in mind you have only yourselves to thank!

REESE: Well, let me tell you something about women. They're always late.

She surprised all the women with her extreme knowledge of scripture when Charlene challenged her minister, who didn't believe women should be allowed to preach.

Other favorite episodes of this season included one in which the ladies redecorated a cruise ship for singles, where Mary Jo and Suzanne competed for the best looking date and noted drag artist Charles Pearce appeared as the shipboard entertainment. This season also introduced Julia and Suzanne's half brother Clayton (Lewis Grizzard), who came for a visit after being released from a mental hospital with the news that he wanted to become a stand-up comic.

Season Two Episodes

101 Ways to Decorate a Gas Station
Written by Linda Bloodworth Thomason
Directed by Harry Thomason
When a bum wins Sugarbaker's promotional contest,
    Charlene fears he's the diamond in the rough her
    psychic predicted she'd marry.

Ted Remarries
Written by Linda Bloodworth Thomason
Directed by Harry Thomason
Mary Jo competes with Ted and his new girlfriend,
    Tammy, for her children's affections.

Anthony, Jr.
Written by Linda Bloodworth Thomason

Directed by David Trainer
A young woman shows up claiming Anthony is the
    father of her baby boy.

Killing All the Right People
Written by Linda Bloodworth Thomason
Directed by Harry Thomason
A fellow designer who is dying of AIDS asks the firm to
    design his funeral.

Half an Air Bubble Off
Written by Linda Bloodworth Thomason
Directed by Harry Thomason
Bernice takes part in a senior citizen beauty contest.

Dash Goff, the Writer
Written by Linda Bloodworth Thomason
Directed by David Trainer
Suzanne's ex-husband shows up in need of inspiration.

Heart Attacks
Written by Linda Bloodworth Thomason
Directed by Matthew Diamond
Reese suffers a heart attack.

Cruising
Written by Linda Bloodworth Thomason
Directed by Harry Thomason
When the ladies redecorate a cruise ship, Mary Jo and
    Suzanne compete to see who can land the best-
    looking man.

I'll Be Seeing You
Written by Linda Bloodworth Thomason
Directed by David Trainer
Charlene falls in love with Colonel Bill Stillfield and
    dreams of a World War II romance.

Stranded
Written by Linda Bloodworth Thomason
Directed by David Trainer
Suzanne and Anthony bond when they are stranded in
    a seedy motel during a blinding snowstorm.

Howard the Date
Written by Linda Bloodworth Thomason
Directed by Harry Thomason
A nerdy guy convinces the women to raise his self-
    esteem by accompanying him to his high
    school reunion.

I'll Be Home for Christmas
Written by Linda Bloodworth Thomason
Directed by Harry Thomason
Suzanne plays a holiday prank that results in the theft of
    everyone's gifts.

Great Expectations
Written by Linda Bloodworth Thomason
Directed by David Trainer
Mary Jo and J. D. introduce their kids. T. Tommy
    Reed shows up wanting Anthony to go into business
    with him.

Second Time Around
Written by Linda Bloodworth Thomason
Directed by David Trainer
Feeling guilty about his deceased wife, Bill breaks up
   with Charlene leaving her devastated.

Oh, Brother
Written by Linda Bloodworth Thomason
Directed by David Trainer
Clayton, Julia and Suzanne's half brother, gets out
   of a mental hospital and wants to become a
   stand-up comic.

There's Some Black People Coming to Dinner
Written by Linda Bloodworth Thomason
Directed by Jack Shea
Mary Jo's daughter is upset when her boyfriend's
   father doesn't want him to date a white girl.

The Return of Ray Don
Written by Linda Bloodworth Thomason
Directed by David Trainer
Suzanne's accountant, Reggie Mac Dawson, absconds
   with her life savings.

High Rollers
Written by Linda Bloodworth Thomason
Directed by Harry Thomason
Suzanne drags Anthony and Charlene to Atlantic
   City in an effort to gamble her way back
   to wealth.

The Incredibly Elite, Bona Fide, Blue-Blood Beaumont
   Driving Club
Written by Linda Bloodworth Thomason
Directed by Matthew Diamond
Suzanne's lifelong dream has been to join the exclusive
   Beaumont Driving Club, but the membership com-
   mittee only wants Julia.

How Great Thou Art
Written by Linda Bloodworth Thomason
Directed by Harry Thomason
Charlene resigns from her church when her minister
   admits he doesn't believe women should be allowed
   to preach.

Ted-Bare
Written by Linda Bloodworth Thomason
Directed by Hal Holbrook
Mary Jo is shocked when her ex-husband Ted makes
   overtures about them getting back together.

Reservations for Eight
Written by Linda Bloodworth Thomason
Directed by Hal Holbrook
When an avalanche closes the slopes during a ski
   weekend, the women and their dates fight the battle
   of the sexes instead.

According to Suzanne Sugarbaker

We all have had heroes who let us down and disappointed us. "I was wild about Anita Bryant. I wanted

to walk like her, talk like her, have her hair. Then she went off on the homosexual thing—became obsessed—stopped showing up at pageants and for what? It wasn't like she was some poor homely girl who had to worry about the homosexuals taking all the good-looking men or anything like that. And you know, the last time I saw her, even her hair looked sorta deflated."

A publicity photo from the hour-long special episode, "The First Day of the Last Decade of the Entire Twentieth Century," in which Charlene's baby is born. (Left to right) Annie Potts, Delta Burke, Dixie Carter, Jean Smart, Dolly Parton, Linda Bloodworth Thomason.

CHAPTER FIVE

Season Three, 1988-1989

THE THIRD SEASON of *Designing Women* introduced writer Pamela Norris, with whom Linda Bloodworth Thomason began to share writing duties. Pamela Norris was from Atlanta and had been a writer on *Saturday Night Live*. Linda says Pam passed her job interview with flying colors by correctly identifying a Stuckey's Pecan Log, a sweet staple of any car trip through the South.

Season three belonged in a large part to Charlene. She convinced the ladies to accompany her on a pilgrimage to Graceland in "E. P. Phone Home" and had to be deprogrammed after getting caught up with a cult-like group of saleswomen in "The Junies." Ultimately, in the fiftieth episode of the series, Charlene and Bill were married, although a bachelor party where Bill was handcuffed to Little Latin Lupe (Fabiano Udenio), an exotic dancer, almost derailed their wedding.

Julia's greatest moment of season three happened off screen, when she got the back of her dress tucked into her panty hose during a charity fashion show, mooning the Mayor and various Atlanta dignitaries. She also ran for tax commissioner, but lost her temper during a televised debate, causing her to lose the election by a landslide. Finally, in the season finale, Julia was so outraged by a local newsstand's display of a poster of a scantily clad woman wearing a dog collar, that she repeatedly drove her car over it.

The season included Mary Jo's quest for larger breasts in "Little Haas and Big Falsie" and the end of her three-year relationship with J. D. Shackleford. Suzanne attempted to recoup some more of her life savings when her accountant, Reggie Mac Dawson, was discovered playing piano and working as a bellboy in a rundown Atlanta hotel. Reggie Mac claimed to have invested Suzanne's money in a circus, out of his desire to see her as Queen of the Big Top. Ultimately, Reggie Mac went on the run again, one step ahead of bouncing checks. Anthony thrilled Suzanne when he was elected homecoming representative of his college.

Alice Ghostley appearances as Bernice continued. She was the highlight of two of the season's best episodes. In one, she believed she was getting married and expected the women to plan her wedding and be her "little flower girls." While Julia, Mary Jo, and Charlene actually have the terrible dresses Bernice had selected fitted, Suzanne collapsed on the couch with hers draped across herself, claiming PMS. As a Christmas gift, Bernice enrolled the ladies in an endurance challenge weekend in the woods, where to everyone's shock, her fog was lifted and she became her group's fearless leader.

Season three included the addition of Meshach Taylor to a new version of the show's opening credits. Each series regular was pictured in several different antique-tinted photographs. This introduction was used through the end of season five and the departures of Delta Burke and Jean Smart from the series.

FAVORITE QUOTES FROM SEASON THREE

From "Tyrone" by Linda Bloodworth Thomason.

MARY JO: You told some guy's parents that he's a bisexual?
SUZANNE: That's right. I always tell the parents. And I'm not sorry either. I don't believe in bisexuals. I figure the rest of us have to choose, so why shouldn't they?

From "The Last Humorously Dressed Bellboy in America" by Linda Bloodworth Thomason.

ANTHONY: What'd you get a ticket for?
SUZANNE: Driving in a reckless manner by having all the mirrors on my vehicle turned towards myself.

Q FACT
All in the Family

Over the course of seven seasons, there were quite a few family members seen on screen that the TV audience knew nothing about. Linda Bloodworth Thomason's niece, Stacy Bloodworth, played the young pageant contestant who does an impression of Jessica Lange in "The Beauty Contest." Only about eight years old at the time, Stacy recalled that her Aunt Linda was always dressing her up as Groucho Marx, teaching her songs and impressions, and putting her on top of pianos to sing. Playing the pageant contestant was just an extension of their endless game of let's pretend.

Delta Burke's mother, Jean Burke, was seen in the congregation of Charlene's wedding. She was seated next to Linda Bloodworth Thomason's real-life uncle, Howard Bloodworth, who played Charlene's uncle and gave a special toast at the wedding. Dixie Carter's daughters, Ginna and Mary Dixie, are probably the most famous family members. Featured in an episode called "The Naked Truth," they played Julia and

Season Three Episodes

Reservations for 12, Plus Ursula
Written by Linda Bloodworth Thomason
Directed by David Trainer

Suzanne's nieces, one as opinionated as Julia, the other as self-absorbed as Suzanne.

The largest role played by a family member went to series Executive Producer Harry Thomason's brother, Danny, who brought life to Suzanne's thieving accountant, Reggie Mac Dawson. Danny joked that it was the largest guest star role written for an optometrist in the history of television. Danny ended up with the part of Reggie Mac when the production needed a photo to use as a wanted poster the first time the character was mentioned. Danny said, "They needed a poster of whoever stole Suzanne's money, so Harry thought it would be great to put my face up there and I think that's how I ended up on the show actually." Later when Linda wanted to write the character into an episode, Danny's face had been well established. In "The Last Humorously Dressed Bellboy in America" the women discovered Reggie Mac working in a rundown Atlanta hotel, where he played cocktail piano. Suzanne confronted him, grabbing his face. Danny remembered, "I talked to Delta Burke's mother and she told me, 'I love the way you let your face go when Delta grabs it.' I wasn't letting it go. She was just grabbing it so hard, it just kinda went on its own."

During a Florida vacation, the women compete with a Swedish au pair bombshell.

The Candidate
Written by Linda Bloodworth Thomason

A FAVORITE QUOTE FROM "COME ON AND MARRY ME, BILL"

Wedding toast:

UNCLE HOWARD: You know, being an old country lawyer, I usually get to deal with the debris of marriage, so it's a high privilege for me tonight to be in on the beginning of a marriage that looks so promising. Bill, Charlene—it's obvious to everybody here the passion that y'all hold for one another. It's something you can't fake, you can't hide, you can't buy; when you got it, you got it. And you two surely have it. My wish for you this evening is that you carry that passion with you through all your remaining days . . . always dancing that great male/female dance of love, sex, marriage, and eternal friendship as no one else has ever danced it before you. May you, in short, dance the *perfect* Missouri waltz.

Directed by David Trainer
Julia runs for tax commissioner.

E. P. Phone Home
Written by Linda Bloodworth Thomason
Directed by David Trainer
Charlene convinces the group to join her on a pilgrim-
    age to Graceland.

Getting Married and Eating Dirt
Written by Linda Bloodworth Thomason
Directed by David Trainer
Bernice is getting married and wants the women to be
    her "little flower girls."

Big Haas and Little Falsie
Written by Linda Bloodworth Thomason
Directed by Harry Thomason
Mary Jo considers using an unexpected inheritance to
    get her breasts enlarged.

Hard Hats and Lovers
Written by Linda Bloodworth Thomason
Directed by David Trainer
Charlene thinks Bill should date some other women to
    make sure she's the right one.

Curtains
Written by Linda Bloodworth Thomason
Directed by David Trainer
The design firm is caught in the middle of a textile
    workers' strike.

The Wilderness Experience
Written by Linda Bloodworth Thomason
Directed by David Trainer
Bernice enrolls the women in a wilderness endurance
    course as a Christmas gift.

Tyrone
Written by Linda Bloodworth Thomason

Directed by David Trainer
Anthony becomes a volunteer Big Brother to a juvenile
  delinquent.

Mr. Bailey
Written by Pamela Norris
Directed by David Trainer
A client leaves her money to her cat.

The Naked Truth
Written by Linda Bloodworth Thomason
Directed by Iris Dugow
The women are hired to redecorate a nudist colony. Julia
  and Suzanne's nieces visit and are younger versions of
  them.

The Junies
Written by Pamela Norris
Directed by David Trainer
Charlene gets caught up selling cleaning products for a
  cult-like organization called Lady June.

One Sees, the Other Doesn't
Written by Pamela Norris
Directed by Ron Troutman
Suzanne dates a blind guy.

Odell
Written by Cassandra Clark and Debbie Pearl
Directed by Dwayne Hickman
Charlene's younger brother elopes with the daughter of
  their father's worst enemy.

Full Moon
Written by Linda Bloodworth Thomason
Directed by David Trainer
Julia moons a large group when she accidentally tucks
    the back of her skirt in her panty hose.

Mr. Meal Ticket
Written by Linda Bloodworth Thomason
Directed by Hal Holbrook
J. D. loses his job and moves in with Mary Jo.

The Engagement
Written by Pamela Norris
Directed by David Trainer
Bill takes Charlene home to meet his upper-crust
    mother and aunt.

Come On and Marry Me, Bill
Written by Linda Bloodworth Thomason
Directed by David Trainer
The wedding almost doesn't happen when Bill and
    Charlene end up handcuffed to an exotic dancer
    named Little Latin Lupe.

The Women of Atlanta
Written by Linda Bloodworth Thomason
Directed by Harry Thomason
A sleazy photographer shoots the women for a men's
    magazine.

Stand and Fight
Written by Pamela Norris

YOU'VE BEEN TERMINATED . . .

From "A Blast from the Past" when a tourist asked Julia if her house had ever been a whorehouse.

JULIA: All right. That's it. This is not a whorehouse, this is *my* house. And I've had all I'm gonna take of you. You don't care about history, you just want to sell it. You don't even sell it honestly. You just want to sell the myth. The myth of the Old South. You all know that myth, don't you? Happy darkies singing in the fields while Miss Scarlet primps around throwing hissy fits. Well that's an insult. It isn't the South. It's an insult to all the people who lived and died here not so very long ago. We Southerners have had to endure many things. But one thing we Southerners don't have to endure is a bunch of bored housewives turning historical homes into theme parks, not to mention ill-mannered tourists with their Big Gulps, Mysties, Slurpees, and Frosties, their dirty feet overflowing rubber thongs, and babies who sneeze fudgecicle juice! Out! Out of my house! As God is my witness, I will burn it down myself before I let you in again!

Directed by David Trainer
After Mary Jo is mugged, the women enroll in a
   self-defense class.

The Last Humorously Dressed Bellboy in America
Written by Linda Bloodworth Thomason
Directed by David Trainer
Reggie Mac Dawson returns to Atlanta with the claim
    he spent Suzanne's money on a circus.

Julia Drives Over the First Amendment
Written by Pamela Norris
Directed by David Trainer
Enraged over a pornographic poster of a woman in a
    dog collar, Julia repeatedly drives her car into it.

Charlene's World War II dream sequence from the episode "I'll Be Seeing You." (Left to right) Delta Burke, Jean Smart, Dixie Carter, Annie Potts, Meshach Taylor.

CHAPTER SIX

Season Four, 1989-1990

TO ACCOMMODATE Jean Smart's own pregnancy, season four began with the explanation that Charlene got pregnant on her honeymoon. Due to the pregnancy, Charlene appeared in fewer episodes. Still, she's integral to "The Rowdy Girls," in which she discovered that her cousin Mavis (Kim Zimmer), was a victim of spousal abuse. In this episode, she also joins the other women, with Suzanne in blackface, in a send-up of the Supremes lip-syncing "Ain't No Mountain High Enough." Charlene's baby was born in a special hour-long New Year's Eve episode entitled "The First Day of the Last Decade of the Entire Twentieth Century." In it, Charlene dreamed of Dolly Parton, her guardian movie star, who told her all about the daughter she's going to meet.

Season four was a grand year for Suzanne. Delta Burke requested that Linda Bloodworth Thomason write a script dealing with her weight gain. The resulting episode, "They Shoot Fat Women, Don't They?" earned Delta an Emmy nomination. In other episodes, Suzanne almost lost her Miss Georgia World crown due

Q FACT: The Guardian Movie Star

Dolly Parton portrayed herself on an hour-long episode called "The First Day of the Last Decade of the Entire Twentieth Century." Charlene was about to give birth to her daughter, Olivia, and she dreamed of a visit from her guardian movie star, Dolly Parton. The episode aired around the same time Parton's movie, *Steel Magnolias*, was released and the women were on the way to see it when Charlene went into labor.

Costume Designer Cliff Chally said Dolly left nothing about her appearance to chance. Dolly brought all her own clothes and when Cliff checked in to see if she needed anything before the filming was to begin, she

to a judge's error, was attacked by fur protesters while wearing a mink pullover in a fashion show, and was shocked to find out an old friend from her pageant days was now a lesbian.

Julia biggest moment of the season happened at her son Payne's spur-of-the-moment wedding. Upset at the idea of becoming a grandmother, Julia drank too much champagne and delivered a sexually charged version of was already completely dressed, hair and makeup all done. She told him, "It takes a lot of money to look this cheap."

Years later in 2003, TV Land started giving awards for classic television shows. Dolly Parton was honored as Best Female Guest Star in a Comedy Series Playing Herself. Dolly beat out two first ladies and a famous psychologist. Nancy Reagan was nominated for her "Just Say No" anti-drug appearance on *Diff'rent Strokes*. Betty Ford was singled out for her 1970 appearance on *The Mary Tyler Moore Show* in which Mary and Lou attend a seminar in Washington D.C. Finally, Dr. Joyce Brothers was nominated for an episode of *Happy Days* in which she deals with Fonzie's depressed dog.

"Sweet Georgia Brown" during the wedding reception. Julia also ended up with her head stuck in the staircase railing of the governor's mansion when she tried to prove to the other women she could act as crazy as they could.

Mary Jo kept looking for love, even going so far as allowing Suzanne to become her romance coach. Anthony fared better in the romance department, dividing

A FAVORITE QUOTE FROM "THE FIRST DAY OF THE LAST DECADE OF THE ENTIRE TWENTIETH CENTURY"

DOLLY: When Olivia comes into the world tomorrow, they'll be with her, everyone in your family who's gone before you, everyone you've loved. . . . You'll see them in her eyes, and her smile, and even the way she walks—and when she says her first words and takes her first step . . . they'll be there. . . . When she has a fever at three o'clock in the morning, when she gets

his time between super yuppie Lita and ghetto fabulous Vanessa, not to mention Suzanne's unending demands. Bernice was back on the scene again when her niece attempted to have her declared incompetent, and almost stole the show from Charlene's new baby when she arrived wearing a Christmas tree skirt. The season closed with the ladies and Anthony visiting a spa, where Charlene and Suzanne were put on diets and Julia and Mary caught in the rain walking home from school, when she hits her first baseball . . . they'll be there.

CHARLENE: Are you sure?

DOLLY: Yes. When she's afraid of the dark, when she forgets to say her prayers, when the wind catches her laugh on a warm summer day . . . they'll be there . . . And just remember, when you meet your daughter tomorrow, on the first day of the last decade of the entire twentieth century, you'll be meeting the person who's going to be holding your hand when it's your time to go. And even then, Charlene, she won't be alone . . . they'll be there.

Jo were urged to fatten up. The resulting mud tub fight got everyone tossed out.

Season Four Episodes

Proxy Pigs and Great Pretenders
Written by Linda Bloodworth Thomason

Directed by Harry Thomason

Anthony hurts his back about the same time Noel the
  pig runs away. Suzanne takes over his care,
  completely running his life.

One Night with You

Written by Linda Bloodworth Thomason

Directed by David Trainer

A lonely terminally ill man who went to high school
  with Julia dreams of spending one romantic evening
  with her.

There She Is

Written by Pamela Norris

Directed by David Trainer

Due to a clerical error, pageant officials attempt to
  revoke Suzanne's Miss Georgia World crown.

Nightmare from Hee Haw

Written by Linda Bloodworth Thomason

Directed by David Trainer

On a trip to the North Georgia woods, the group is
  attacked by Daddy Jones and his hillbilly sons.

The Girlfriend

Written by Pamela Norris

Directed by David Trainer

Anthony is being pressured by his new yuppie
  girlfriend who expects him to become the black
  Donald Trump.

The Rowdy Girls
Written by Linda Bloodworth Thomason
Directed by David Trainer
Charlene's cousin Mavis is being physically abused by
her husband.

Bernice's Sanity Hearing
Written by Linda Bloodworth Thomason
Directed by David Trainer
Bernice's niece attempts to have her declared incompetent.

Julia Gets Her Head Stuck in a Fence
Written by Pamela Norris
Directed by David Trainer
While decorating the governor's mansion, Julia gets her
head stuck in a banister railing.

Julia and Suzanne's Big Adventure
Written by Pamela Norris
Directed by Dwayne Hickman
Julia and Suzanne attempt to visit their mother in
Japan, but everything goes wrong.

Manhunt
Written by Pamela Norris
Directed by David Trainer
Suzanne becomes Mary Jo's dating consultant to make
up for denting her car.

They Shoot Fat Women, Don't They?
Written by Linda Bloodworth Thomason

Directed by Harry Thomason
Suzanne's feelings are hurt by comments made by old
    friends at her high school reunion about her
    weight gain.

You Got to Have Friends
Written by Pamela Norris
Directed by David Trainer
Mary Jo takes a job at a fast food restaurant when Ted
    gets behind on his child support payments.

The First Day of the Last Decade of the Entire Twentieth
    Century (hour-long episode)
Written by Linda Bloodworth Thomason
Directed by Harry Thomason
Charlene's baby is born on New Year's Eve.

The Mistress
Written by Linda Bloodworth Thomason
Directed by Iris Dugow
The women are outraged by a client who hires them to
    decorate for both his wife and his mistress.

The Fur Flies
Written by Pamela Norris
Directed by Hal Holbrook
Suzanne is injured by fur protestors at a fashion show.

Oh, What a Feeling
Written by Paul Clay
Directed by David Trainer

When the company van dies on the side of a highway, the ladies find themselves at the mercy of a car salesman.

Anthony and Vanessa
Written by Linda Bloodworth Thomason
Directed by David Trainer
Suzanne coaches Vanessa on how to land Anthony.

Payne Grows Up
Written by Pamela Norris
Directed by David Trainer
Payne graduates from college and marries his pregnant girlfriend, making Julia feel older than she would like.

Tornado Watch
Written by Linda Bloodworth Thomason
Directed by William Crain
A tornado takes part of the roof off the design firm.

Tough Enough
Written by Pamela Norris
Directed by David Trainer
The women bowl against an all-male design firm for the job of redecorating a bowling alley.

It's a Wonderful Life
Written by Thom Bray and Michael Ross
Directed by David Trainer

The women recreate Charlene and Bill's first date in an effort to restart the romance in their marriage.

Foreign Affairs
Written by Cheryl Bascam
Directed by David Trainer
Suzanne pays Anthony to impersonate her maid, Consuela, who is about to be deported.

Suzanne Goes Looking for a Friend
Written by Dee LaDuke and Mark Alton Brown
Directed by David Trainer
Suzanne rekindles an old friendship from her pageant days, not knowing the woman has since come out of the closet.

Have Faith
Written by Pamela Norris and Paul Clay
Directed by David Trainer
Mary Jo feels ill at ease when she dates a minister.

Anthony's Graduation
Written by Linda Bloodworth Thomason
Directed by David Trainer
Mistaking him for a prowler, Suzanne shoots Anthony on the eve of his college graduation.

La Place Sans Souci
Written by Linda Bloodworth Thomason
Directed by Iris Dugow
Suzanne treats everyone to a spa weekend, but a huge fight in a mud tub gets them kicked out.

According to Suzanne Sugarbaker

"I think it's a big fallacy that having too many material things ruins your character. There's no reason that Mother Teresa couldn't be doing the exact same work with orphans if she drove a Mercedes. And that Gandhi—always sitting around in a big diaper—would have been just as effective in a suit and tie."

From "Full Moon," Suzanne prepares to defend Noel the pig.

CHAPTER SEVEN

Season Five, 1990–1991

SUZANNE WAS SEEN less and less in what would be her fifth and final season on the show. She was hysterical when she accidentally purchased Anthony in a charity bachelor auction and then had to have a private dinner with him in her home. Anthony met his long-lost father when Charlene convinced the women to hire a private investigator as a surprise for Anthony's birthday. Much to Suzanne's dismay, Anthony was invited to join the exclusive Beaumont Driving Club. Anthony realized the club only wanted him so they could qualify as a stop on the PGA tour, but he still intended to make the most of his membership.

It was another big season for Charlene. She briefly quit work when she thought she was missing all of baby Olivia's big important firsts, but soon returned, working at home part-time via computer. She also flirted with a modeling career for Olivia. Suzanne, who thought Olivia didn't have enough hair, had one of her own hairpieces cut down to make a baby wig. Charlene also bought a house she believed was haunted, went back to college, and handled Bill being sent to the Persian Gulf. We were treated to a sequel to Charlene's

THE BITCHY BOYS

Designing Women had no shortage of bitchy male characters. In "The Return of Ray Don," wealthy curmudgeon Wilmont Oliver, who Suzanne briefly considered marrying for his money, was accompanied by an attendant. Roland was played in all his vicious glory by Dalton Cathey, who died of AIDS in December of 1990. Roland was only too happy to provide all the gruesome gossip surrounding Wilmont's money-grubbing children and the treachery they had in store for Suzanne if she succeeded in cutting in on their inheritance. Roland began his harangue in true Joan Rivers fashion, gushing, "Can we talk!?"

Charles Pierce, a self-proclaimed male actress possessing the dead-on comedy timing of Bea Arthur, was prominently featured as Claude LaBelle in "Cruising." In the episode, the women were hired to redecorate a cruise ship where Pierce worked as everything from luggage handler to female impersonating entertainment. Suzanne was convinced he had stolen her hairpieces, recognizing her own wig when Pierce appears as Joan Collins. He also did impressions of Bette Davis

World War II dream in "Keep the Home Fires Burning." Mary Jo was still a cigarette girl; this time Julia sang "White Cliffs of Dover" and Anthony impersonated Sergeant Bilko.

and Katharine Hepburn. About his career Pierce had this to say: "I'd like people who see my work to remember me as an actor. A good actor who made his living by doing some really good impressions. The fact that I went from rags to bitches was just one of those quirks of fate written in the stars."

Another fan favorite was the character of Billy Baldwin from the episode entitled "The Incredibly Elite, Bona Fide, Blue Blood Beaumont Driving Club." Billy was described in the script as an effete, impeccably tailored gadfly. Tom Fitzpatrick remembered being cast as Billy about forty-five minutes before the first table read (when the entire cast and crew assembled for the first time to read the week's script). He prodded Anthony by asking him if he was related to Jacqueline Bouvier Kennedy. He also regaled the group with a story of how his ancestors recreated their checkered family history in order to be accepted into Beaumont. Tom said that earlier in the week there had been another scene with Anthony in which he talked about an awful time at the Beaumont Driving Club, when all the kitchen help went out of control and got caught doing the Watusi. The scene was later cut.

Julia was thrilled when her home was included on the historical society's tour, until the actual huddled masses start trooping through. She briefly lived a double life, singing at an Atlanta nightspot called the Blue

Note under the name Giselle. Her biggest hurdle of the season was the untimely death of longtime companion, Reese Watson.

Bernice tried her hand at public access television when she took over as host of *Senior Roundup*. Later, when plastic surgery she had on her nose left her looking like Miss Piggy, no one had the heart to tell her. Mary Jo's search for romance seemed never ending. She briefly dated a man who had initially asked out her daughter Claudia. Mary Jo finished the season with the realization that she wanted to have another baby before it was too late.

Season Five Episodes

A Blast from the Past
Written by Pamela Norris
Directed by David Trainer
Julia is thrilled to have her house included on the
historical society's tour, at first.

Papa Was a Rolling Stone
Written by Cassandra Clark and Debbie Pearl
Directed by David Trainer
Charlene convinces the women to locate Anthony's
father as a surprise for his thirtieth birthday.

Working Mother
Written by Pamela Norris
Directed by David Trainer

Charlene decides to quit when she misses too many of
Olivia's firsts.

Miss Trial
Written by Dee LaDuke and Mark Alton Brown
Directed by David Trainer
Julia is sequestered with a jury when Charlene reports
her for discussing the case.

The Bachelor Auction
Written by Pamela Norris
Directed by David Trainer
Suzanne accidentally buys a date with Anthony at a
charity auction.

Charlene Buys a House
Written by Pamela Norris
Directed by David Trainer
Charlene hires the women to decorate her new house,
which she believes is haunted.

Old Rebels and Young Models
Written by Dee LaDuke and Mark Alton Brown
Directed by Iris Dugow
Mary Jo's art teacher comes to stay when she runs
away from her nursing home. Charlene tries to
start Olivia on a career in modeling, complete with
baby wig.

Nowhere to Run To
Written by Cassandra Clark and Debbie Pearl

Directed by David Trainer
Julia becomes obsessed with jogging. This is the series
   one-hundredth episode.

A Class Act
Written by Cassandra Clark and Debbie Pearl
Directed by Dwayne Hickman
Charlene decides to go back to college.

Keep the Home Fires Burning
Written by Dee LaDuke and Mark Alton Brown
Directed by David Trainer
When Bill is deployed, Charlene attends a support
   group for soldiers' spouses and has a sequel to her
   World War II dream.

My Daughter, Myself
Written by Pamela Norris
Directed by David Trainer
Mary Jo goes out with a man who was too old to date
   her daughter, Claudia.

And Now, Here's Bernice
Written by Dee LaDuke and Mark Alton Brown
Directed by David Trainer
Bernice tries her hand at a public access show called
   Senior Roundup.

Pearls of Wisdom
Written by Pamela Norris
Directed by David Trainer

Mary Jo loses a strand of pearls that belong to Suzanne, not knowing they are fake.

High Noon in a Laundry Room
Written by Dee LaDuke and Mark Alton Brown
Directed by David Trainer
The laundry room in Anthony's building has become a hangout for a biker gang, forcing Anthony to take it back.

How Long Has this Been Going On?
Written by Cassandra Clark and Debbie Pearl
Directed by David Trainer
Julia is secretly singing in an Atlanta nightclub.

The Emperor's New Nose
Written by Thom Bray and Michael Ross
Directed by David Trainer
When Bernice's plastic surgery goes wrong no one wants to tell her.

Maybe Baby
Written by Pamela Norris
Directed by David Trainer
Mary Jo wants to have another baby.

This Is Art?
Written by Steve Roth and Deanne Roth
Directed by Roberta Sherry-Scelza
Julia becomes the darling of the Atlanta art scene after accidentally selling a purse.

Blame It on New Orleans
Written by Dee LaDuke and Mark Alton Brown
Directed by David Trainer
At a design convention, Mary Jo has a fling, then finds
out the man is married.

YOU'VE BEEN TERMINATED . . .

Julia confronted a sleazy photographer in "The Women of Atlanta."

JULIA: I'm saying I want you and your equipment out of here now. If you are looking for somebody to *suck pearls*, then I suggest you try finding yourself an oyster. Because I am not a woman who does that; as a matter of fact, I don't know any woman who does that, because it's stupid. And it doesn't have any more to do with decorating than having cleavage and looking sexy has to do with working in a bank. These are not pictures about the women of Atlanta. These are about just the same thing they're always about. And it doesn't matter whether the clothes are on or off, it's just the same ol' message. And I don't care how many pictures you've taken of movie stars. When you start snapping photos of serious, successful businessmen like Donald Trump and Lee Iacocca in unzipped jumpsuits with wet lips, straddling chairs, then we'll talk.

I'll See You in Court
Written by Cassandra Clark and Debbie Pearl
Directed by David Trainer
Mary Jo sues the guy who mugged her.

The Big Circle
Written by Pamela Norris
Directed by David Trainer
Reese Watson dies from a heart attack. Randa Oliver's
    parents abandon her with Julia.

Friends and Husbands
Written by Cassandra Clark and Debbie Pearl
Directed by David Trainer
Bill returns from the Middle East, as Charlene
    and Mary Jo are finishing up with their first
    children's book.

Fore!
Written by Pamela Norris
Directed by David Trainer
In an attempt to become a stop on the PGA tourna-
    ment, the Beaumont Driving Club offers Anthony
    a membership.

The Pride of Sugarbaker's
Written by Thom Bray and Michael Ross
Directed by Iris Dugow
Julia and Mary Jo coach Randa and Quint's little
    league team.

Taken following the filming of "Reservations for Eight,"
on Valentine's Day. (Front row, left to right) Annie Potts,
Richard Gilliland, Jean Smart, Doug Barr, Dixie Carter,
Hal Holbrook. (In back) Delta Burke, Gerald McRaney.

CHAPTER EIGHT

Season Six, 1991-1992

WITH ALL THE PUBLICITY surrounding the departure of Delta Burke at the end of season five, the TV audience couldn't wait to see who would be stepping in to fill the shoes of Suzanne Sugarbaker, and, as it turned out, Charlene Stillfield as well. The premiere episode of season six drew an audience of over thirty million viewers. Written by Linda Bloodworth Thomason, the sixty-minute season kickoff introduced Sugarbaker cousin and new partner, Allison (Julia Duffy), and Charlene's never-mentioned sister, Carlene Dobber (Jan Hooks).

Jean Smart decided, after five seasons, to pursue other acting challenges, so Charlene and Bill were transferred to London. Charlene does show up for the first episode to pave the way for her sister, the newly divorced Carlene Dobber. In previous seasons, Charlene had made mention of sisters Marlene, Harlene, and Darlene, who was the maid of honor at her wedding. Carlene was a new creation, much less sophisticated than her sister, much more the hick. Unfortunately, the character came off as cartoony and a bit shrill. It almost seemed that taking the *H* out of Charlene's name, took the heart out of the similar character.

Never having left their hometown of Poplar Bluff, Carlene was awestruck by everything to do with the big city of Atlanta. Carlene had married Dwayne Dobber (Ray McKinnon) right out of high school. Dwayne claimed to be the number one import car salesmen in all of southeast Missouri, a title he lorded over Carlene as proof of his superior level of sophistication. In contrast, Carlene shared plenty of stories about Dwayne playing "pull my finger" and expecting her to serve drinks to his business associates wearing hot pants. When Dwayne showed up in Atlanta, Carlene used him as a sex object, but had become smart enough not to get pulled back into a relationship.

Carlene fancied herself a songwriter. Her song, "Atlanta, Where My Sweet Dreams Come True" actually became a finalist in an Olympic theme song competition. Unfortunately, most of Carlene's songs fell into the category of "Remember the Good Old Days. They were good. They were old. They were days."

Mary Jo Shively became a surrogate big sister to Carlene, taking her out for her first trip to a singles bar. By contrast, Allison treated Carlene like a charity case, establishing the Allison Sugarbaker College Fund to pay Carlene's tuition. In return, Allison expected to have total control of Carlene's life.

If Allison Sugarbaker had her way, she would control everyone's life. After buying out Suzanne's interest in the design firm, Allison showed up claiming a controlling interest in the company. Played perfectly by Julia Duffy, the character of Allison seemed somewhat reminiscent of the role of Stephanie that she had created for the *Newhart* show.

Dominating, self-centered, and diagnosed with OPD (obnoxious personality disorder), Allison moved in with a giant desk and started attempting to run Sugar-baker's like a huge corporation. She wanted regular hours, permanent records, and questioned Charlene for bringing Olivia to work. Allison was also in a War of the Roses–type battle with Anthony over Suzanne's house. Suzanne leased her mansion to both of them and neither was willing to budge.

Before moving to Atlanta, Allison lived in New York City where she was employed as a seeing-eye person for a wealthy blind woman who was allergic to dogs. After spending a year with the firm, Allison took her cash to invest in a Victoria's Secret franchise.

The sixth season started with a continuation of Mary Jo's quest to become pregnant, in an effort to write Annie Potts' real-life pregnancy into the story line. Unfortunately, it was the same season Vice President Dan Quayle made comments regarding unwed mother Murphy Brown's pregnancy on the show that immediately followed *Designing Women* on Monday nights. After one unsuccessful attempt at the sperm bank, Mary Jo's pregnancy went on the back burner and Annie Potts was forced to spend most of the season hiding her own pregnancy, even missing several episodes toward the end of the season.

This season gave us one of the most famous episodes of the entire series run, "The Strange Case of Clarence and Anita." It was also one of the only times in history a situation comedy made such a direct and timely comment on a current political issue. The episode was set amid the confirmation hearing of Supreme Court nominee Clarence Thomas and the sexual harassment accusations made by Anita Hill. Julia and Mary Jo were in full support of Anita Hill. Allison sided with Clarence Thomas. All hell broke loose in the midst of Allison's birthday party, with Julia and Mary Jo costumed as Joan Crawford and Bette Davis for a little theater production of *Whatever Happened to Baby Jane?* and everyone gave their opinions to a local news reporter.

After the death of Reese Watson, Julia began to re-enter the dating scene, first dating Mark Bayswell (Charles Frank), a man she assumed was gay because of his interests in musical theater and close relationship with his mother. (Totally Useless Trivia: Charles Frank played the first of Erica Kane's numerous husbands on *All My Children*.) Later in the season, Julia allowed herself to be talked into a birthday date with lonely Rusty (Michael Goldfinger), the firm's longtime electrician who can never seem to keep his pants pulled up.

Bernice's arterial flow seemed to decrease to a trickle this season. She developed a strange crush on Anthony, complete with a song, "Black Man, Black Man," that she sang whenever he was near. Over the top or not, the performance earned a Best Supporting Actress Nomination for Alice Ghostley.

Anthony continued his law school studies, was harassed by racist mall cops while shopping with Bernice, and ended the season with the announcement that he intended to marry a new client, the uberwealthy Vanessa Chamberlain (Jackee Harry).

A FAVORITE QUOTE FROM "THE STRANGE CASE OF CLARENCE AND ANITA"

BERNICE: And I'll tell you another thing. That Anita Bryant has caused trouble before when she went out against the homosexuals. And here she is, trying to ruin this man.

ANTHONY: Bernice, that was Anita Bryant, this is Anita *Hill*.

BERNICE: Oh. Well I thought Anita Bryant was white, but they both have the same hairdo.

Season Six Episodes

The Big Desk (hour-long episode)
Written by Linda Bloodworth Thomason
Directed by Harry Thomason
Allison Sugarbaker buys Suzanne's share of the business
    and wants to run things like a huge corporation.
    Charlene's sister, Carlene, takes over as office
    manager when Charlene and Bill are transferred
    to England.

Q FACT: Sugarbaker Clients: The Few, The Crazed

For a show set in an interior design firm, very little interior decorating took place. When clients did show up, they were usually a little off, causing Mary Jo to wonder on more than one occasion if the women were playing fast and loose with their own sanity.

Lamar Tyson was a sort of combination prude and maniac, asking for a canvas halter top for the fire hydrant in front of his house and little cloth strips for the naked figures in his religious paintings. Julia draws the

A Toe in the Water
Written by Pamela Norris
Directed by David Steinberg
Julia is dating a man she believes is gay.

Dwayne's World
Written by Dee LaDuke and Mark Alton Brown
Directed by David Steinberg
Carlene's ex-husband comes for a visit.

Marriage Most Foul
Written by Dee LaDuke and Mark Alton Brown

line at aluminum foil on the walls of his home, but does agree to find a fabric for his sofa that doesn't include too much sexual activity.

Tony and Cassandra Hall were known as the most repulsive couple in America. They are rich Beverly Hills white trash who have moved to Georgia. They enjoy plastic surgery and discuss their endless sex lives with anyone who will listen.

The Roscoe-Baileys were a megawealthy couple who drove around Atlanta in their Rolls-Royce dressed up like the police when they weren't at home playing nudist colony. When B. J. Poteet moved to Atlanta and bought a furnished mansion that came with a bondage room, it turned out to have belonged to the Roscoe-Baileys.

Directed by David Steinberg
Allison is left at the altar by a man she turned in for insider trading.

Picking a Winner
Written by Dee LaDuke and Mark Alton Brown
Directed by Asaad Kelada
Mary Jo uses a sperm bank in her effort to have a baby.

Last Tango in Atlanta
Written by Thom Bray and Michael Ross

Directed by Charles Frank
Anthony convinces the women to participate in a prison
   outreach program and everyone ends up in the
   middle of a prison riot.

The Strange Case of Clarence and Anita
Written by Linda Bloodworth Thomason
Directed by David Steinberg
The Sugarbaker women take sides on the controversial
   confirmation hearings of Supreme Court nominee
   Clarence Thomas and Anita Hill's accusation of
   sexual harassment.

Just Say Doe
Written by Andrea Carla Michaels
Directed by David Steinberg
Mary Jo's brother, Skip, is attracted to Allison.

Julia and Rusty Sittin' in a Tree
Written by Thom Bray and Michael Ross
Directed by David Steinberg
Julia agrees to a birthday date with Rusty, the firm's
   electrician.

Julia and Mary Jo Get Stuck Under a Bed
Written by Linda Bloodworth Thomason
Directed by David Steinberg
While investigating their competition in a Christmas
   decoration contest, Mary Jo and Julia end up hiding
   under a bed while an endless sex romp goes on over
   their heads.

Real Scary Men
Written by Cathryn Michon
Directed by David Steinberg
The women crash a men's sensitivity weekend.

Tales Out of School
Written by Pamela Norris and Paul Clay
Directed by David Steinberg
Anthony tries to take advantage of his law professor's
    attraction to Carlene.

Driving My Mama Back Home
Written by Dee LaDuke and Mark Alton Brown
Directed by William Cosentino
Mary Jo and Julia accompany Mary Jo's mother on her
    bus trip home following bunion surgery.

Payne Comes Home
Written by Eleanor S. Hyde-White
Directed by Paul Clay
Julia is thrilled to have Payne home for a visit until it
    seems to be a permanent situation.

Carlene's Apartment
Written by Paul Clay
Directed by David Steinberg
Carlene rents her first apartment in the seediest part
    of Atlanta.

Mamed
Written by Dee LaDuke and Mark Alton Brown

Directed by David Steinberg
Julia takes over Anthony's little theater production of
   Mame.

A Scene from a Mall
Written by Dee LaDuke and Mark Alton Brown
Directed by David Steinberg
Anthony is racially profiled at a local mall.

All About Odes to Atlanta
Written by Dee LaDuke and Mark Alton Brown
Directed by David Steinberg
Carlene is a finalist in an Atlanta theme song
   contest.

I Enjoy Being a Girl
Written by Norma Safford Vela
Directed by David Steinberg
The women sponsor a group of very spoiled
   girl scouts.

L.A. Story
Written by Paul Clay
Directed by Roberta Sherry-Scelza
When Allison invests in a movie, the women and
   Anthony join her on a trip to Los Angeles.

A Little Night Music
Written by Linda Bloodworth Thomason
Directed by David Steinberg
While in the hospital, Julia is romanced by
   her doctor.

Shades of Vanessa
Written by Linda Bloodworth Thomason
Directed by Art Dielhenn
The women are stunned when Anthony announces his
    plan to marry Vanessa Chamberlain and make her a
    very vocal partner in their business.

CHAPTER NINE

Season Seven, 1992-1993

THE SEVENTH AND FINAL SEASON began with the news that Allison had pulled her money out of Sugarbaker's in order to buy a Victoria's Secret franchise, leaving the business in a precarious financial situation. Allison's replacement, B. J. Poteet, played by Judith Ivey, was introduced as a wealthy new client who ended up a new partner in the business after a drunken poker game with Julia.

B. J. met and married wealthy contractor James Poteet while working as a court reporter in Houston, Texas. Unfortunately, their life together ended tragically when he died of a heart attack during their wedding reception. James did make B. J. an extremely wealthy widow and the president of Poteet Industries. B. J. liked to claim her family never liked James, accusing him of marrying her for her sense of humor.

It wasn't unusual for B. J. to buy expensive gifts for her new coworkers or offer to fly them around the country at the drop of a hat. B. J. was very conservative, especially compared to liberal Julia, and never tired of needling her.

YOU'VE BEEN TERMINATED . . .

Julia's first termination of the series, from the pilot episode. She destroyed Ray Don Simpson in the Tokyo Gardens sushi bar.

RAY DON SIMPSON: Allow me to introduce myself, Ray Don Simpson.
JULIA: There's no need for introductions, Ray Don, we know who you are.

Most of the season focuses on Anthony's wedding to Vegas showgirl, Etienne Toussaint (Sheryl Lee Ralph). To raise Anthony's spirits after being dumped by Vanessa Chamberlain, B. J. flies the entire group to Sin City. Anthony, in a drunken haze, marries Etienne. At first, he was horrified by what he'd done, but later decided to try to make the marriage work.

Mary Jo and Julia finally squared off in an episode entitled "Mary Jo vs. the Terminator." Later everyone struggled to make it to Washington for President Bill Clinton's inauguration. The other major change of season seven was the addition of Alice Ghostley as a regular cast member, appearing in over half of the season's twenty-two episodes.

Sadly, *Designing Women* slipped from its firm place among the top twenty highest rated television shows

RAY DON SIMPSON: You do?

JULIA: Of course. You're the guy who is always wherever women gather or try to be alone. You want to eat with us when we're dining in hotels, you want to know if the book we're reading is any good, or if you can keep us company on the plane. And I want to thank you, Ray Don, on behalf of all the women in the world, for your unfailing attention and concern. But read my lips and remember, as hard as it is to believe, sometimes we like talking just to each other, and sometimes we like just being alone.

when CBS moved it from its normal Monday time period to a slot on Friday nights. This resulted in a mediocre hour-long, season-ending episode, where each of the women fantasized about being Scarlet O'Hara in *Gone with the Wind*, which became the finale to the entire seven-season run. When asked in various interviews how she might end *Designing Women,* Linda Bloodworth Thomason always joked that Anthony and Suzanne would finally fall in love and run off together in the ultimate marriage of Old South and New South. While the final moments of the series are not Anthony and Suzanne, the last scene did feature Bernice's fantasy in which Anthony, dressed as Rhett Butler, carried Bernice, costumed as a hoop-skirted Scarlet, up the grand staircase of Tara while she sang "Black Man, Black Man" at the top of her lungs. There was an appropriate symmetry to this scene since Anthony and Bernice made their first *Designing Women* appearances together in the season one episode, "Perky's Visit."

This time when cancellation was announced, there was no fan outcry, letter-writing campaign, or rallying attempt to save the show. By the second half of the seventh season, due to behind-the-scenes changes in the writing staff, *Designing Women* had become like a beloved old friend who was hooked up to life support. One might not have wanted to pull the plug, but sadly it was obvious the time had come.

Season Seven Episodes

Of Human Bondage
Written by Linda Bloodworth Thomason
Directed by David Steinberg
The women play poker with a wealthy client, B. J.
    Poteet, who wins a share of their business.

Sex and the Single Woman
Written by Dee LaDuke and Mark Alton Brown
Directed by David Steinberg
Carlene uses her ex-husband as a sex object.

Mary Jo vs. the Terminator
Written by Dee LaDuke and Mark Alton Brown
Directed by David Steinberg
Mary Jo stands up to Julia for the first time in
    their friendship.

On the Road Again
Written by Dee LaDuke and Mark Alton Brown
Directed by David Steinberg
Mary Jo, Julia, and Bernice take off for Memphis on the
    spur of the moment.

Screaming Passage
Written by Norma Safford Vela
Directed by David Steinberg
Julia enters menopause.

Viva Las Vegas
Part one written by Linda Bloodworth Thomason
Part one directed by Charles Frank
Fools Rush In
Part two written by Linda Jean LaBrown
Part two directed by David Steinberg
Anthony joins the women on a getaway to Las Vegas
    where he impulsively marries showgirl Etienne.

Love Letters
Written by Norma Safford Vela
Directed by David Steinberg
B. J. is upset by a steamy love letter from another
    woman she finds in her late husband's deposit box.

The Vision Thing
Written by Norma Safford Vela
Directed by David Steinberg
Etienne's attempts to become the perfect wife drive
    Anthony crazy.

Trial and Error
Written by Robert Horn and Danny Margosis
Directed by David Steinberg
Law student Anthony tries to help Mary Jo with her
    small claims court case.

Too Dumb to Date
Written by Jeannie Elias
Directed by David Steinberg
Mary Jo dates a "himbo."

The Odyssey
Written by Dee LaDuke and Mark Alton Brown
Directed by David Steinberg
Everything goes wrong as the women attempt
    to make their way to President
    Clinton's inauguration.

Oh, Dog, Poor Dog
Written by Cathryn Michon
Directed by David Steinberg
Bernice thinks the bad news she overhears about Mary
    Jo's dog being put down is about her.

Wedding Redux
Written by Mimi Pond
Directed by David Steinberg
Anthony and Etienne restage their wedding for
    Etienne's parents and Anthony's grandmother.

Nude Julia, New York Morning
Written by Emily Levine

Q FACT: The Claudia Foundation

Linda Bloodworth Thomason founded the Claudia Foundation in 1989 in honor of her mother, who died of transfused AIDS. The foundation is headquartered in the Bloodworth House, the home of Linda's paternal grandparents. Located in Linda's hometown of Poplar Bluff, Missouri, the Bloodworth House is used for various social, educational, and cultural events.

The Claudia Foundation has awarded Designing Women Scholarships in excess of a million and a half dollars, making it possible for young women to attend Duke University, Vanderbilt University, Wellesley College, and many other higher education institutions across the United States.

The foundation also sponsors the Charlie Classics Reading Program in honor of Linda's grandfather, Charles T. Bloodworth. The program encourages high school students to read one hundred literary masterpieces before graduation. Students are encouraged to select books from a list created by Linda Bloodworth Thomason and English teachers and librarians from Poplar Bluff schools. After reading each classic, students are required to discuss the book with a trained volunteer adult mentor. This student/adult interaction promotes positive relationships between generations. Furthermore, the Claudia Foundation awards scholarships to each Poplar Bluff senior who has read one hundred approved books before graduation.

AN HONOR JUST TO BE NOMINATED AND NOMINATED AND . . .

Over the seven-season run, *Designing Women* was nominated for numerous awards. Casting Director Fran Bascom was nominated for Best Casting for a Television Comedy by the Casting Society of America in 1987, 1989, and 1990. The Directors Guild of America nominated Harry Thomason in 1990 for directing "They Shoot Fat Women, Don't They?" The Hollywood Foreign Press singled out the show for Best Comedy Series nominations in 1990 and 1991. The Academy of Television Arts and Sciences honored *Designing Women* with seventeen Emmy nominations. Alice Ghostley was nominated for Best Supporting Actress in 1992. Meshach Taylor was nominated for Best Supporting Actor in 1989. The series itself was nominated for Best Comedy Series in 1989, 1990, and 1991. Cliff Chally was nominated for Costume Design four times. Delta Burke was nominated for Outstanding Actress in a Comedy in 1990 and 1991. Linda Bloodworth Thomason was nominated for writing "Killing All the Right

Directed by David Steinberg
A mentor from Julia's art school days in New York
  unveils his nude portrait of her.

People." The show also received nominations for Outstanding Multiple Camera Editing, as well as Outstanding Sound Mixing. And in 1988, *Designing Women* actually received an Emmy for Outstanding Achievement in Hairstyling for the episode "I'll Be Seeing You." This episode contained Charlene's World War II dream sequence.

The show may not have won many Emmys, but other organizations were much more generous. The now defunct Viewers for Quality Television chose *Designing Women* as Best Quality Comedy Series for its first four seasons. The show was also honored by the Center for Population Options for demonstrating sexual responsibility in the media with their Nancy Susan Reynolds Award, and the Alliance for Gay and Lesbian Artists in the Entertainment Industry (AGLA) bestowed its media Award of Merit. In addition, the series won numerous GLAAD Awards (Gay & Lesbian Alliance Against Defamation), as well as Angel Awards presented by Excellence in Media, a California-based organization dedicated to the promotion of quality family-oriented programming. Finally, the County of Los Angeles Board of Supervisors gave the show a special commendation for producing "The Rowdy Girls" and for its efforts on behalf of the Domestic Violence Council.

Sex, Lies and Bad Hair Days
Written by Robert Horn and Danny Margosis
Directed by David Steinberg
B. J. swears off men after her birthday is filled with bad
    blind dates.

Shovel Off to Buffalo
Written by Emily Levine
Directed by David Steinberg
When the face of Elvis appears on Mary Jo's snow
    shovel, she believes she has the power to heal people.

It's Not So Easy Being Green
Written by Emily Levine
Directed by David Steinberg
Anthony is wildly jealous of Etienne's old friend.

The Woman Who Came to Sugarbaker's
Written by Emily Levine
Directed by David Steinberg
A visit from Julia's former head mistress seems endless
    until the ladies stage a séance to force her to leave.

The Lying Game
Written by Robert Horn and Danny Margosis
Directed by David Steinberg
Carlene's new boyfriend is a cross-dresser.

Gone with a Whim (hour-long episode)
Written by David Steinberg, Robert Horn, and Danny
    Margosis
Directed by David Steinberg
While redecorating a house that resembles Tara, the
    ladies fantasize about being Scarlet in *Gone with the
    Wind*.

CHAPTER TEN

The Q Friendliest Episodes

"Killing All the Right People"
Written by Linda Bloodworth Thomason
Directed by Harry Thomason
Original airdate October 5, 1987

Filmed on August 12 of 1987, *Designing Women* was the first situation comedy to deal head-on with AIDS and the homophobia that was rampant at the time. The episode aired on October 5 of that same year. *The Golden Girls* followed in February of 1990 with an episode called "72 Hours" in which Rose was told she may have contracted the HIV virus through a blood transfusion after an operation. In April of 1991, Whoopi Goldberg guest starred in an episode of *A Different World* called "If I Should Die Before I Wake." Whoopi received an Emmy nomination for Outstanding Guest Actress in a Comedy Series for the show, which dealt with a student who revealed she contracted AIDS through unprotected sex in high school.

In "Killing All the Right People," Kendall Dobbs (Tony Goldwyn), a young decorator and friend of Sugarbaker's, discovered that he was dying of AIDS. He asked the ladies to design his funeral. The ladies agree to redecorate a room in a local funeral home in the style of New Orleans' French Quarter. When a client, Imogene Salinger, overheard the plans, she was appalled, telling the women she thought people with AIDS were getting what was coming to them. Julia put her in her place quickly and pointed out that if God were giving out sexually transmitted diseases for sinning then everyone would be constantly at the free clinic. At the same time, Mary Jo became involved in a controversy at Claudia's school over giving condoms to students. Although she didn't want Claudia to have sex at an early age, Mary Jo realized that the safe sex issue was about "preventing deaths, not births." In her speech to the PTA, Mary Jo described her friend who was dying and explained that regardless of the moral issues involved, teenagers shouldn't have to die for their actions. Her speech was met with huge applause. The episode closed with the ladies, Anthony, and Bernice attending Kendall's funeral as a Dixieland band plays a jazz version of "Just a Closer Walk with Thee."

Camilla Carr portrayed Sugarbaker client Imogene Salinger, and had the difficult task of telling the women she thought AIDS was "killing all the right people." Camilla recalled that several actresses had been offered the part ahead of her, but turned it down because they did not want to play such an unsympathetic, evil character. Camilla, who produced the original run of "Last Summer at Bluefish Cove" starring Jean Smart, was already well aware that the AIDS epidemic had started. Many of her friends had already become ill and been diagnosed. She saw the role of Imogene as her opportunity to "help get the word out about how AIDS and HIV could be contracted and how it affected people" and is still flattered today when people tell her how much they hated her in the part.

An urban legend has grown around this episode, claiming that the role of Kendall Dobbs was originally to be portrayed by an actor with AIDS, but during the weeklong rehearsal period, the actor became too ill to play the part. There is no truth to this story. Casting Director Fran Bascom saw quite a few young actors for the part, among them Tony Maggio and Rob Knepper, who gained fame playing the role of T-Bag on *Prison Break*. Ultimately Tony Goldwyn, a few years before his evil turn in *Ghost*, landed the role.

The Beauty Contest
Written by Linda Bloodworth Thomason
Directed by Jack Shea
Original airdate October 6, 1986

A FAVORITE QUOTE

SUZANNE: This just makes me furious! You know, when men use Women's Liberation as an excuse not to kill bugs for you. Oh, I just hate that! I don't care what anybody says, I think the man should have to kill the bug!
JULIA: I don't think I can add anything to that.

YOU'VE BEEN TERMINATED . . .

Julia confronted Imogene Salinger in "Killing All the Right People."

IMOGENE: I don't care what you say, Julia Sugarbaker, I believe this is God's punishment for what they've done . . . I just know that these people are getting what they deserve!
JULIA: Imogene, get serious! Who do you think you're talking to? I've known you for twenty-seven years, and all I can say is, if God was giving out sexually transmitted diseases to people as a punishment for sinning, then you would be at the free clinic all the time! And so would the rest of us!

The second episode of *Designing Women* contained what is considered by many to be the best of all of Julia's Terminator speeches. Suzanne was depressed over her upcoming thirtieth birthday and Charlene had submitted Mary Jo's daughter's picture for the Miss Pre-Teen Atlanta Contest. Mary Jo didn't want Claudia to participate, but eventually gave in. Suzanne overcame her birthday blues by becoming Claudia's pageant coach. Claudia became a contest finalist, but eliminated herself when she admitted to the judges she had only been giving answers she thought they wanted to hear instead of being herself. Julia overheard the current Miss Georgia World, Marjorie Lee Winnick, making fun of how Suzanne had given a two-hour lecture at a recent pageant on "Manners, Cuss Words, and How Not to Cross Your Legs" and share a joke that the long-missing Jimmy Hoffa had been found in Suzanne's big hair. Julia set her straight in what most consider to be her finest Terminator speech of all time. Pamela Bowen, who portrayed Marjorie Lee Winnick, recalled how unnerved she was by Dixie's portrayal. backstage before filming the big scene, Pamela remembered asking Dixie how she kept her skin looking so beautiful. The two bonded over skin care regimes with Dixie espousing her reliance on the rough hotel washcloths she always used to scrub off dead cells. After chatting like girlfriends, they had to do the big tell-off scene. Pamela said, "Dixie went from so sweet and nice and down to earth to going out and scaring me. She almost made me cry." Dixie Carter recalled that Linda told her she'd had the speech whipping around in her head long before writing the episode. "Linda wanted Julia to say that about her sister after picking at each other and arguing—to make a turn so that the audience could see for itself the deep love and loyalty there—which is what made *Designing Women* what it was in my opinion."

The Wilderness Experience
Written by Linda Bloodworth Thomason
Directed by David Trainer
Original airdate January 9, 1989

For Christmas, Bernice enrolled the ladies in a wilderness experience weekend. Not wanting to hurt her

YOU'VE BEEN
TERMINATED . . .

From "The Beauty Contest" by Linda Bloodworth Thomason, the speech below is recited word for word in gay
bars across the country and is considered by many to be
Julia's finest moment.

JULIA: I'm Julia Sugarbaker, Suzanne Sugarbaker's
sister. I couldn't help overhearing part of your
conversation . . . I gather from your comments there
are a couple of things you don't know . . . For example,
you probably didn't know that Suzanne was the only
contestant in Georgia pageant history to sweep every
category except congeniality. And that's not something
the women in my family aspire to anyway. Or that
when she walked down the runway in her swimsuit,

feelings, they are forced to participate. Divided into
teams, Bernice, Suzanne, and Charlene are joined by
Dorothy and Evelyn, two sweet, elderly ladies, reminiscent of the Baldwin sisters on *The Waltons*. Julia and
Mary Jo find themselves teamed with Big Edie, Mickey
Junior, and Corrine. Big Edie and Mickey Junior were
tough garment workers from New York City who fancied themselves a couple of "urban cowgirls" out to take
in the big horizon. They were rude and domineering.
After trying to cope with them for a day, Julia and Mary
Jo take off on their own. Lost in the woods and discov-

five contestants quit on the spot . . . Or that when she emerged from the isolation booth to answer the question, "What would you do to prevent war?" she spoke so eloquently of patriotism, battlefields, and diamond tiaras, grown men wept . . . And you probably didn't know that Suzanne wasn't just any Miss Georgia. She was the Miss Georgia! She didn't twirl just a baton. That baton was on fire. And when she threw that baton into the air, it flew higher, further, faster than any baton had ever flown before, hitting a transformer and showering the darkened arena with sparks . . . and when it finally did come down, my sister caught that baton and twelve thousand people jumped to their feet for sixteen and one-half minutes of uninterrupted, thunderous ovation, as flames illuminated her tear-stained face. And that, Marjorie, just so you will know, and your children will someday know, is the night the lights went out in Georgia!

ering a pay phone, they called Anthony for emergency assistance. Anthony arrived with food and a new tent. While he was inside securing the new tent, the wilderness experience leader arrived. Anthony quickly put on a lady's hat and scarf and pretended to be one of the campers. When the weekend finally ended, Julia and Mary Jo were shocked to find out Bernice's group had been the most successful and Bernice had earned the highest leadership rating.

Doris Hess, who showed up in *Beaches* as Barbara Hershey's housekeeper, played Mickey Junior. She explained that she was named Mickey Junior for her father, who really wanted a boy and was very disappointed when she came along, to which Julia responds, "Why?" After overhearing Suzanne attempting to hire someone to carry her on a hike, Big Edie remarked that she'd love to get her hands on Suzanne, claiming she'd make a real woodsman out of her. Julia assured Big Edie that Suzanne saw the Ned Beatty scene in *Deliverance* and probably wouldn't be interested in anything she had in mind.

Big Edie was portrayed in her swaggering glory by Denny Dillon. Currently living in New York's Hudson Valley in a little town called Stone Ridge, Denny still acts and, at the same time, runs her own art gallery out of her 1840s restored farmhouse. "I opened my art gallery in May of 2005. I basically moved back east because I missed New York. After living in Los Angeles for about eight and a half years, I moved back east and lived in New York on 57th Street in a condo. And loved being back in New York, did my comedy act, did lots of theater." Denny's artwork can be seen at www.thedraw ingroomonline.com.

On filming the episode, Denny recalled, "It looked like outdoors, but all was filmed inside the studio. My memories are all joyous. I was thrilled to be on the show because I'm a big fan of the show. What I remember, they asked me to be on the show, but I didn't know what my part was because they hadn't written the script yet. And I was on a TV show at the time—that was November 1988. I had been on *Women in Prison*. They were gonna write something for me and model it after my character Meg Bando on *Women in Prison.* And I said yes and was thrilled."

The part of the mousy housewife Corrine was played by Maggie Murphy, who had recently moved to Los Angeles with a friend who was also one of Annie Pott's best friends. On the set, when Annie learned of their connection, she insisted that episode director David Trainer give Maggie lots of great close-ups. Maggie went on to work as an executive in David Kelley's company during *Ally McBeal* and *The Practice.* Currently, she is the president of Kiefer Sutherland's production company.

This was also the episode where Anthony was caught attempting to help Julia and Mary Jo by bringing them food and a new tent in the middle of the woods. He disguised himself with some of their clothes and the result is the quote on the next page.

Suzanne Goes Looking for a Friend
Written by Dee LaDuke and Mark Alton Brown
Directed by David Trainer
Original airdate April 9, 1990

Suzanne had tickets for a charity event and, after being turned down by the other three ladies, decided it was time to find a new friend. After searching through her address book, Suzanne called Eugenia Weeks (Karen Kopins Shaw), a woman from her pageant days. Eugenia, a local weather reporter, attended the event with Suzanne and they had a wonderful time. When Eugenia stopped by Sugarbaker's the following day, the other ladies quickly realized she was gay. Suzanne thought

A FAVORITE QUOTE

CONNIE: What's this camper's name?
ANTHONY *(in a high-pitched voice)*: Cindy.
CONNIE: Cindy what?
ANTHONY: Cindy Birdsong.
CONNIE: Birdsong? I don't remember that name. *(to other leader)* Check your list.
ANTHONY: I was late. I got on the bus at the last minute.
CONNIE: Who let you on?
ANTHONY: I don't know. Some white girl.

"coming out late" meant she was a very old debutante. Suzanne immediately became concerned that Eugenia was falling in love with her. Attempting to ignore the entire friendship, Suzanne went into hiding at her health club, but Eugenia tracked her down. An older woman, overhearing their conversation, made derogatory comments about Eugenia and Suzanne came to her defense. Suzanne decided to continue their friendship, figuring at least they wouldn't cut into each other's territory.

Karen Kopins Shaw is vastly different from the role of Eugenia Weeks. Retired from acting, she's married and living in Connecticut with four children. "My daughter was just accepted on the U.S. snowboard team.

She just turned sixteen. And my sons, they're all following in the same footsteps. They're all number one in the United States, all four of them. So, we'll see what happens." Karen had no qualms about playing the lesbian character and feels she and Delta had a great chemistry together. "I really liked working with her. She was just so friendly and down to earth and took me under her wing and brought me into her dressing room. What an actress—comedically, she's so good. She's so trained. It just felt so natural to play that character."

The writers of the episode, Dee LaDuke and Mark Alton Brown, also have great memories. While living in New York, Mark and Dee, a gay man/straight woman writing team, sold a spec script to *Designing Women*. In it Noel the pig ate the cremated remains of Suzanne's greatest pageant mentor just hours before they were to be scattered at a memorial service. The episode was never produced and "Suzanne Goes Looking for a Friend" became their introduction to series television. Dee remembered the night the episode aired: "The switchboard lit up. Linda said, you'd think this woman—I know gay people need role models, but you'd think this woman cured cancer the way the switchboard lit up with gay people across the country saying you've got to bring Eugenia back. People were that desperate for a reflection of somebody who was gay on television." Dee and Mark received a GLAAD award for writing this important episode.

Foreign Affairs
Written by Cheryl Bascom

A FAVORITE QUOTE

SUZANNE: If they can put a man on the moon, I don't see why we can't put one on you.

Directed by David Trainer
Original airdate April 30, 1990

Suzanne bribed Anthony into posing as Consuela for immigration officials when her maid's work permit expired and she was forced to take a citizenship test. Meanwhile, Sugarbaker's gets stuck with an Arabian Knights gel-filled bed, custom ordered for Tony and Cassandra Hall, "the most repulsive couple in America," who refused to pay.

In the tradition of such invisible characters as Vera on *Cheers* and Maris on *Frasier*, the fact that Suzanne's maid, Consuela Valverde, is never seen made her all the more outrageous. During the run of the series, she put curses on both Suzanne and Charlene and had a huge crush on Anthony. Playing Consuela was one of the times Meshach Taylor ended up in full drag on the show. Meshach recalls, "I liked playing Consuela because I got to do my little accent and everything. And plus, there was something intrinsically very comedic about this black man trying to be this Spanish lady and pulling it off."

Cruising
Written by Linda Bloodworth Thomason

Directed by Harry Thomason
Original airdate November 16, 1987

While attending career day at Anthony's old high school, Julia and Mary Jo met a travel agent who told them about a cruise line that was looking for a decorating firm to refurbish its flagship. Sugarbaker's accepted the job and the ladies took the cruise to determine what needed to be done. Once on board, Mary Jo was angered by Suzanne's belief that every man on the ship was after her. As a result, Mary Jo and Suzanne had a contest to see who could take the handsomest man to the captain's dinner at the end of the cruise. Suzanne met Trevor, a very handsome male version of herself. After spending a romantic evening with him, Suzanne

A FAVORITE QUOTE

CHARLENE: I wonder what's keeping Anthony and Suzanne.
JULIA: Charlene, are you serious? A six-foot black man dressed like Hazel just left here with Suzanne, his co-conspirator to defraud and deceive the United States government, and you're wondering what's keeping them? Well, it's been three and a half hours. I don't think you have to wonder anymore. I think it's pretty obvious. They are in prison.

decided she was truly in love. The next morning at breakfast, Trevor made a pass at Mary Jo. She realized that going along with him would allow her to win the bet, but she refused to betray Suzanne. She informed Trevor that he was too dumb to appreciate Suzanne, "the Rolls-Royce of females." Mary Jo and Suzanne left the ship realizing they had each made new friends in each other.

The Rowdy Girls
Written by Linda Bloodworth Thomason
Directed by David Trainer
Original airdate October 30, 1998

Charlene's cousin Mavis helped the ladies prepare to play the Supremes in the Decorative Arts Center talent show, but Charlene was devastated to accidentally discover that her beloved childhood companion was the victim of spousal abuse. Meanwhile, Suzanne upset everyone when she showed up to perform in blackface makeup.

Series Costume Designer Cliff Chally remembered making the ladies sparkling Supremes costumes. Since time was usually a factor, Cliff had many tricks and shortcuts that made outfits look great on camera quickly. "In order to make a gown look like it was beaded on camera, you can use Elmer's Glue and glitter. You just put Elmer's Glue right on the chiffon and then throw glitter on it and when it dries and you see it on film, it looks just like it has been beaded . . . We were out in the parking lot with those chiffon things spread out and I was drizzling glue and throwing glitter all over."

Blame It on New Orleans
Written by Mark Alton Brown and Dee LaDuke
Directed by David Trainer
Original airdate March 4, 1991

In New Orleans for Design Expo, Mary Jo gave in to a long-standing flirtation with Garret Rossler (Darrell Larson), a gentleman acquaintance, and was devastated the morning after to discover he was a married man. Suzanne and Charlene explored the entire city. Suzanne became confrontational with drag queen Lolita DuPage (David Shawn Michaels), insisting she was really a man pulling a *Victor/Victoria* type scam. This resulted in a showdown in which both pulled off their wigs and finally exited to the ladies room to settle the matter once and for all. Suzanne ran out moments later, screaming, "There's a man in the ladies room!"

Mamed
Written by Dee LaDuke and Mark Alton Brown
Directed by David Steinberg
Original airdate February 3, 1992

Anthony was chosen to direct a community theater production of *Mame* and convinced the ladies to audition. To everyone's delight, Julia won the lead, drawing the ire of lushy former Broadway actress Ivy McBride who was producing the show and was used to getting all the lead roles. She was cast as Mame's friend Vera instead. On opening night, Ivy went on a bender and Anthony was forced to play the role of Vera, singing "Bosom Buddies" with Julia. Mary Jo was cast as Mame's homely assistant, Agnes Gooch, whose sack-like costumes were perfect for hiding Annie's real-life pregnancy. This was another full drag opportunity for Meshach Taylor; this time Vera Charles had a strong resemblance to Pearl Bailey.

All About Odes to Atlanta
Written by Mark Alton Brown and Dee LaDuke
Directed by David Steinberg
Original airdate March 2, 1992

In an homage to *All About Eve*, Carlene entered a contest to write the official theme song for Atlanta, with Julia and Mary Jo helping her sing it. Carlene was delighted by all the attention she got from her groupie, the mousy Heather. Allison and Anthony never trusted Heather. The night of the contest, the ladies discovered that Heather was a contestant as well and considered them her biggest competition.

A Toe in the Water
Written by Pamela Norris
Directed by David Steinberg
Original airdate September 23, 1991

Upset at being locked overnight in the basement of Suzanne's house, Anthony threatened Allison with legal action. Obtaining an affidavit from his law school professor asserting his right to occupy the house, Anthony gave Allison two choices, either move out or stay on as his personal servant. Meanwhile, after meeting Julia's new romance, Mark Bayswell (Charles Frank), Allison

A FAVORITE QUOTE

CARLENE: Haven't you ever noticed that your top celebrities either have big heads or big hair? If you have a big head like Michelle Pfeiffer, you don't need big hair. But if your head's little tiny like Dolly Parton, then you need big hair to compensate.

insisted that Julia was only comfortable dating him because he is so obviously gay. After a night at the symphony, Julia returned with Mark to his apartment where he made a pass at her. Julia was forced to admit that deep down she really did believe he was gay. The two finally agreed to continue only a friendship.

The Lying Game
Written by Daniel Margosis and Robert Horn
Directed by David Steinberg
Original airdate May 7, 1993

Carlene's new boyfriend, Eric, seemed too good to be true. The fact that he was often unavailable and often secretive made the others suspect that he might be married. When they confronted Eric, he showed up dressed as a woman. Trying to understand Eric, Carlene dressed up as a man—just in time to stand up to a male chauvinist client.

CHAPTER ELEVEN

Why Do We Love Thee? Let's Count the Ways!

1. We Love Unpredictable, Over-the-Top Behavior

From *The Women* to *All About Eve*, who can resist outrageous behavior and bitchy banter? Julia, Suzanne, Mary Jo, and Charlene had colorful opinions about everything and they never held back. Jean Smart remarked, "I think traditionally gay men are attracted to women who are bigger than life. Starting with Judy Garland and Joan Crawford and right on up to Bette Midler—women who are out there, who don't follow traditional mores of the time. This is especially true of Dixie and Delta's characters. Julia was traditional, but did not suffer fools."

TV Guide Senior Editor Matt Roush had this to say: "*Designing Women* is one of the landmarks I think for vivid character comedy in all of television. It was also a pressure cooker because the language on the show would sort of reach boiling levels sometimes. I mean, pre-dating Dennis Miller, you had all these women who'd go off on these major rants, especially Julia Sugarbaker. It was before people were doing snaps, which is a part of the jargon today, but I mean, the snaps came off of their tongue because they were just so full of vinegar, and they just wouldn't, y'know, they just wouldn't play dead for anybody."

Series Writer Mark Alton Brown added that *Designing Women* "celebrates its eccentrics. It is very similar to the gay sensibility which celebrates eccentricity, celebrates the individual, and the more outspoken, the more wild you are, the funnier you are."

The character of Suzanne Sugarbaker cornered the market on eccentricity. Julia claimed that the hardest work notoriously sedentary Suzanne had ever done was attempting to blow dry her hair exactly the same way her hairdresser did. As a child, her coloring books only had the hair filled in, and she once sent an autographed photo of herself to a friend of her mother's after backing over his dog at a party.

Annie Potts agreed that gay men are drawn to larger-than-life characters. Annie also pointed out that straight men are constantly admitting to her that they liked the show, "like they're ashamed that it appealed to them—these strong, smart, sassy women. But gay men were unabashedly approving. And I guess gay men relate more like women in the fact that we're a minority and that we've both been put down. And once we're in our own group, we're emboldened and we get to say what we really think and be who we really are. We have a lot in common that way. When the macho men aren't listening, we're really much more our real selves and we [straight women and gay men] are really the most interesting people on the planet."

Dixie Carter believes it took more than just an outlandish sense of humor to attract the support and attention of the gay community. Dixie believed "the wit that was there was acerbic, yes, but there was also a depth of heart and some real sweetness between the characters that I think is essential to become popular with the gay community, to be received with that kind of enthusiasm. That wit we associate with plays about gays—that kind of 'I'm gonna take you down and slice you up,' that's not the kind of thing that scores unless it is accompanied by substance. There must be some depth of heart or it's not going to really land." Dixie's opinion supports the continuing popularity of the show, which has never been out of reruns since cancellation. *Murphy Brown*, a show that started at roughly the same time as *Designing Women* and won tons of Emmys, doesn't seem to have the same long-term appeal, possibly because it was very heavy on wit and humor, but light on heart.

2. The Extremely Literary Style

Linda Bloodworth's writing is a calling card all on its own. Noted dialogue coach, Eva Charney said, "If Dorothy Parker, Noel Coward, and Eudora Welty had a spectacular three-way, their resulting love child would be Linda Bloodworth Thomason. Because of her dazzling writing and the world she created in *Designing Women,* we could always tune in and see this loving party going on."

When other situation comedies were churning out the typical formula, Linda devoted whole shows to a study group formed to help Anthony pass his college literature class. It may possibly be the only sitcom where characters discussed *The Great Gatsby*'s symbolism and irony—even if Suzanne spent most of the debate cleaning out her purse.

Meshach Taylor believes "it is the repartee between the women. It's the conversation. It's really reminiscent of the best of the gay writers we have. The way Linda writes puts you in mind of Noel Coward, of even sometimes Tennessee Williams. The way language was used in a very descriptive manner that can go on for a while, rather than just back and forth in dialogue. Someone could speak for two or three or four or five sentences and get a good run going. I think that's something the more literate minds in the gay community picked up on."

Series writers Dee LaDuke and Mark Alton Brown believed that writing for *Designing Women* took a special sensibility that very few people in Hollywood had. Mark believes "Linda has this heightened sense of the absurd that I think runs through Southern culture and Southern literature." Dee LaDuke adds, "It's a natural hyperbole you're kind of born with and that's why the South may not be the most tolerant place on earth, but it tolerates individuals. And that's why people like Truman Capote could be Truman Capote, growing up where he did. Those kind of individuals come out of the South. And I don't just mean the gay individual spirit, but the eccentric, as well." Mark Alton Brown continues, "I think if you can write a show that appeals to women and gay men, you've got a hit. Other people will come along for the fun."

Designing Women continues to age very well. Even today, the writing remains as crisp, fast, unpredictable, and spot-on funny as anything else on television. It has a voice all its own.

3. An Irresistible Cast

The original four ladies had a dynamic balance that, along with Meshach Taylor and Alice Ghostley, kept us coming back for more. Writer Mark Alton Brown believes that finding actresses who are both beautiful and funny was as rare as finding gold.

Delta Burke believes the cast of *Designing Women,* "was like a little band. Everyone has a different note to play, and we all came together and made music."

Jeff Sagansky, the former president of CBS remarked, "*Designing Women* probably had one of the all-time memorable ensemble casts. It ranks right up there with *The Mary Tyler Moore Show* and *Cheers.*" And Matt Roush, *TV Guide* senior editor added, "Each and every one of these designing women is a complete star in her own right. As an ensemble, they're almost unparalleled."

4. A Family One Wanted to Join

Designing Women, where the politics were always progressive, stressed the importance of a chosen family. The way these characters chose each other and supported each other was inspiring and life affirming, especially at a time in the late eighties when, according to Dialogue Coach Eva Charney, she was "losing a friend every two weeks to AIDS."

The cast of *Designing Women* shared life's milestones, both on camera and off. When Richard Gilliland started playing J. D. Shackleford, Mary Jo's love interest, early in the first season, Jean Smart found him attractive. She asked Delta Burke to discreetly find out if he was involved with anyone. In true Delta fashion, she shouted across the soundstage, "Excuse me, Richard! Do you have a girlfriend? Jean wants to know if you're married." He wasn't and on June 7, 1987, Jean Smart and Richard Gilliland were married in a beautiful garden wedding at the home of Dixie Carter and Hal Holbrook.

Jean discovered she was expecting the same night Charlene's wedding was filmed. Ronnie Claire Edwards, who played Charlene's mother, Ione, on *Designing Women,* and Corabeth Godsey, the shopkeeper's wife on *The Waltons*, hosted a fantastic baby shower for Jean in her beautiful Los Feliz home.

It was in the second season that Gerald McRaney appeared on the show as Dash Goff, Suzanne's first ex-husband and possibly the great love of her life. Casting Director Fran Bascom recalls that the list of actors considered for the role included everyone from Dack Rambo to Randy Quaid. Initially, Gerald's agents said he was very interested but not available due to a family conflict. Fortunately, the situation changed and he was able to play Dash. Delta admits to being immediately smitten during the filming of his first episode. About their first on-camera kiss, Delta said, "I remember that kiss because I forgot my lines." Gerald McRaney remembers "I had taken one look at those blue eyes and I was gone. I was just gone." He asked Delta out for a drink after work and Annie Potts tagged along. She waited until Delta had excused herself for a moment and leaned across the table to Gerald and said, like any big sister, "Now listen, if you mess with her, I'm gonna kill you." Delta and Mac's romance progressed and he sent her white roses, Delta's favorite flower, with a card message that made Delta fall in love. It said: "In Mississippi, there is a section of the state studded with antebellum homes, rich in both beauty and substance. It is so fertile that when one simply casts seeds onto the soil, it will sprout and flourish and bring new life in the enchanted place called the Delta." Delta and Mac were married on May 28, 1989, in a lavish ceremony that made the cover of *People* magazine. Dixie Carter was Delta's Matron of Honor and the entire cast was in attendance.

On the final episode of *The Mary Tyler Moore Show*, Mary made a speech about what constituted a family. She said, "I get to thinking my job is too important to me, and I tell myself that the people I work with are just the people I work with. And not my family. And last night, I thought, 'what is a family, anyway?' They're just people who make you feel less alone . . . and really loved. And that's what you've done for me. Thank you for being my family." Mary's words are just as relevant when applied to the family of *Designing Women*. In spite of anything one may have read, they were a family—on stage and off—a real family with ups and downs, eccentricities, and lots of love.

CHAPTER TWELVE

The Cast's Favorite Episodes

How Great Thou Art
Written by Linda Bloodworth Thomason
Directed by David Trainer
Original airdate February 22, 1988

Dixie Carter's favorite episode was "How Great Thou Art." It was the last episode of the series that Dixie's mother saw in her life. Dixie said, "Linda must have been prescient in that she wrote the show and I got to sing 'How Great Thou Art.' She couldn't have known of the terrible illness that struck my mother, ending her life. I was standing beside her in the hospital room in San Francisco, holding her hand. Can you imagine the feeling my mother had in her heart with her little girl on the screen singing that wonderful old Methodist hymn—it was a gift beyond counting the price."

In the episode, Julia and Charlene were attending a religious conference. Julia was selected to sing "How Great Thou Art" at the closing ceremony, but feared that she didn't have the voice to hit the required high notes. Charlene was upset to learn that her minister was opposed to women in the ministry. She invited Reverend Nunn (Patrick Tovatt) to dinner and was shocked when Bernice successfully debated the issue of women in the ministry, intelligently citing verses of scripture in support of her argument. The ladies were unable to change Reverend Nunn's view and after much soul searching, Charlene resigned from her church. Charlene explained to her minister that, as a small child, she had wanted to be a minister herself. At the last minute, Julia decided not to sing, but Charlene changed her mind. She explained that Julia was her hero and that she needed to be proud of women. Dixie claims to have been as nervous as Julia about hitting the high C. If the letters she still receives about the episode are any indication, Dixie sang the song gloriously.

Jean Smart also claimed this as one of her personal favorite episodes. It showcased Charlene's childlike side and illustrated how she always stood up for what she believed was right. Jean believed the gay community could identify with a desire for fundamental liberties: "To me, one element to a community that still battles for the basic freedom to be themselves, to live their lives, these characters are very appealing."

They Shoot Fat Women, Don't They?
Written by Linda Bloodworth Thomason
Directed by Harry Thomason
Original airdate December 11, 1989

In addition to "Dash Goff, the Writer," the episode when Delta first met Gerald McRaney, her favorite show was the one dealing with her weight issues. Los Angeles

A FAVORITE QUOTE

CHARLENE: . . . you're my hero.
JULIA: Heroine.
CHARLENE: Even better.

Daily News Entertainment Journalist Greg Hernandez also picked this as his favorite episode. He was very moved by a conversation between Julia and Suzanne the morning after Suzanne's high school reunion: "Julia told Suzanne, 'In the end all that matters is what was true and truly felt.' As a closeted gay man [at the time], it really resonated with me. It was something to go on and to try to live by."

In the show, Suzanne was forced to re-evaluate her life when she became the victim of cruel jokes and hurtful comments about her weight gain. When her classmates voted her Most Changed, it was a truly changed Suzanne who accepted the award. Julia and Mary Jo joined Anthony in a food fast to focus attention on world hunger. Suzanne commented that in a world where many people worry about their next meal, she worried about having too much to eat.

Big Haas and Little Falsie
Written by Linda Bloodworth Thomason
Directed by Harry Thomason
Original airdate December 12, 1988

In Annie Potts' favorite episode, Mary Jo's great uncle Dude passed away and left her three thousand dollars with the stipulation that she had to spend it on something frivolous. Mary Jo admitted that she always wanted to have some cosmetic surgery, but always felt too decadent spending money that way. Suzanne immediately guessed what Mary Jo would want to have done and Mary Jo finally admitted she'd like to have larger breasts. Suzanne, of course, had the name of "the best breast man in Atlanta" and dared Mary Jo to make an appointment. Goaded, Mary Jo contacted the doctor and, after learning the surgery cost exactly three thousand dollars, decided to go through with the procedure. The doctor gave Mary Jo several prosthetic bras so she could make a decision about what size she would like to be. Suzanne was concerned that she get her money's worth. Mary Jo discovered that a larger bust size, like alcohol, made her feel aggressive, almost macho. She believed she was the center of attention. While Mary Jo was having the time of her life planning who to point her huge chest at next, everyone else was being driven crazy. Finally, her kids convinced her to spend the inheritance money on TV telephones, a gift for everyone.

In "Little Haas and Big Falsie," series Costume Designer Cliff Chally remembered using silicone boobs that were used by patients after having mastectomies to create the weight and movement of actual breasts.

During the run of the series, Mary Jo manifested a fascination with large breasts. She referred to the nurses ex-husband Ted hired to work in his office as having "life-threatening boobs." She was constantly amazed by the size of Suzanne's chest, admitting during a trip to the beach in "Reservations for Twelve" to putting bras she found drying in the bathroom on her head. Suzanne's cups fit her head like a beanie, but those of Ursula, the Swedish bombshell who had been hired to watch the children, covered Mary Jo's entire face.

Come On and Marry Me, Bill
Written by Linda Bloodworth Thomason
Directed by David Trainer
Original airdate April 10, 1989

Jean Smart selected "Come On and Marry Me, Bill" as her other favorite episode because she found out during the filming that she was expecting her first child.

In the episode, preparations for Charlene's wedding were in full swing. Her bachelorette slumber party was to be held at Suzanne's house until Consuela had a fire in the kitchen. Julia happily volunteered her own home, happy at the mere thought of sleeping in her own bed. A *This Is Your Life* evening was prepared for Charlene, complete with skits and songs. Julia, Mary Jo, and Suzanne sang "My Buddy" to a tearful Charlene. After the wedding rehearsal, Bill's friends and Charlene's brothers had a bachelor party with all the trimmings. One of the trimmings is Little Latin Lupe (Fabiana Udenio), an exotic dancer who spoke only Spanish. She was dancing on a table when she playfully handcuffed herself to Bill with a pair of ménage a trois cuffs. She discovered too late that she didn't have the key. Reese and Anthony called locksmiths and welders, but no one could remove the cuffs. Concerned about her brothers, Charlene arrived and discovered her future husband chained to an exotic dancer. In the resulting uproar, Little Latin Lupe put the third cuff on Charlene. Charlene was forced to get ready for her wedding while cuffed to the dancer and Bill. Monette, Charlene's hooker friend, showed up to do her makeup and had a key in her purse that fit the cuffs. The episode ended with a beautiful wedding montage and Julia singing "Ave Maria."

Stranded
Written by Linda Bloodworth Thomason
Directed by David Trainer
Original airdate December 7, 1987

The ladies had great plans for attending Design Expo in St. Louis which coincided with the Miss Missouri World pageant Suzanne was judging. Julia, Mary Jo, and Charlene flew to St. Louis, but all three came down with a bad case of the flu and spent the first few days of the convention sick in bed. A terrible snowstorm closed the Atlanta airport and Suzanne was forced to ride to St. Louis in the van with Anthony, who was bringing Sugarbaker's design display. Suzanne and Anthony made it to Tennessee before the roads became impassable and they were forced to seek shelter. The Bates Motel had only one room available and Suzanne didn't think it would look right for Anthony to share it with her. Anthony tried to sleep in the van, but eventually the freezing temperature forced him to insist on sharing the room with Suzanne. Suzanne and Anthony had their first real conversation. The snowstorm delayed their arrival in St. Louis and Anthony had to help Suzanne get ready for the pageant. Julia, Mary Jo, and Charlene listened in shock as the two of them prepared for the evening like old friends.

Meshach Taylor recalled that the episode "was fun because that was the first time we got to work together in that kind of close situation." Delta Burked pointed out that it was very common for Linda Bloodworth to pick up on things she hadn't pictured before and then put them into the writing. Delta and Meshach had been sent out on the road together to promote the show and had become tight friends. Linda picked up on their growing friendship and used it for their hysterical characters.

CHAPTER THIRTEEN

Son of *Designing Women*

IN 1995, two years after the lackluster finale of the series, Delta Burke and Linda Bloodworth Thomason decided to join forces once again and *Women of the House* was born. Delta was back again as Suzanne Sugarbaker, this time set in Washington as she took over the seat in the House of Representatives of her deceased fifth husband. This time around Suzanne had a mentally challenged brother Jim (Jonathan Banks) and an adopted Asian daughter Desiree (Brittany Parkyn), who seemed based on the Li Sing character from "Oh, Susannah." At the office, Suzanne was supported by her administrative assistant, Natalie Hollingsworth, played by Patricia Heaton. Teri Garr was Press Secretary Sissy Emerson and Valerie Mahaffey and Julie Hagerty both took shots at the role of Office Secretary Jennifer Malone.

The series ran for only half a season with each episode written by Linda Bloodworth and directed by Harry Thomason. Fans of *Designing Women* were treated to visits from Dash Goff (Gerald McRaney) when he came into town after writing a tell-all book about their

Q FACT: Broadway Bound

If the schedules of all involved can ever be worked out, *Designing Women* will become a Broadway play. Written by Linda Bloodworth Thomason, a play based on the series will be updated, taking into account the time that has passed since the end of the original. Also, the play will leave room for weekly changes so it will be topical and reflect the news of the day. The plan is for Elizabeth Williams and Anita Waxman to produce. The majority of the cast are no strangers to Broadway. Delta and Dixie both appeared in *Thoroughly Modern Millie*. Dixie received rave reviews in a production of Terrence McNally's *Master Class* and Jean Smart was featured with Nathan Lane in a revival of *The Man Who Came to Dinner*.

marriage. Anthony also showed up in an episode called "Dear Diary." Now a lawyer, with no mention of wife, Etienne, Suzanne expected Anthony to dispose of a diary that had been subpoenaed.

The short-run series closed with a powerful episode about the dangers of violence against women in television and film. The episode used well-known Hollywood actresses to testify before Congress as themselves. Participating in the episode were Roseanne Barr, Elizabeth

Ashley, Rita Moreno, Loni Anderson, Shirley Jones, Brett Butler, Joan Van Ark, Stefanie Powers, and Marilyn Chambers.

Women of the House Episodes

Miss Sugarbaker Goes to Washington (hour-long episode)
Written by Linda Bloodworth Thomason
Directed by Harry Thomason
Suzanne decides to take over her deceased husband's seat in the House of Representatives.

Guess Who's Sleeping in Lincoln's Bed?
Written by Linda Bloodworth Thomason
Directed by Harry Thomason
Excited about spending the night at the White House, Suzanne jumps on Lincoln's bed, breaking a slat.

That's What Friends Are For
Written by Linda Bloodworth Thomason
Directed by Harry Thomason
Sissy Emerson is kicked out of her apartment and comes to live with Suzanne and her brood.

Men Are Good
Written by Linda Bloodworth Thomason
Directed by Harry Thomason
Jennifer Malone is terrified at the thought of her first date since her divorce.

YOU'VE BEEN TERMINATED . . .

Julia runs for commissioner, but loses during a televised debate.

WILSON BRICKETT: You heard that, Caller. She just called you ignorant and prejudice!
JULIA: I do not think everyone in America is ignorant! Far from it. But we are today, probably, the most uneducated, under read, and illiterate nation in the western hemisphere. Which makes it all the more puzzling to me why the biggest question on your small mind is whether or not little Johnny is gonna recite the Pledge of Allegiance every morning! I'll tell you something else, Mr. Brickett. I have had it up to here with you and your phony issues and your Yankee Doodle yakking! If you like reciting the Pledge of Allegiance every day then I think you should do it. In the car! In the shower! Wherever the mood strikes you! But don't try to tell me

You Talk Too Much
Written by Linda Bloodworth Thomason
Directed by Harry Thomason
Natalie thinks Sissy poisoned Senator Helms during a
    luncheon.

Bad Girl
Written by Linda Bloodworth Thomason
Directed by Harry Thomason

when or where I have to say or do or salute anything, because I am an American too, and that is what being an American is all about! And another thing, I am sick and tired of being made to feel that if I am not a member of a little family with 2.4 children who goes just to Jerry Fallwell's church and puts their hands over their hearts every morning that I am unreligious, unpatriotic, and un-American. Because I've got news for you, Mr. Brickett, all liberals are not kooks, any more than all conservatives are fascists. And the last time I checked, God was neither a Democrat, nor a Republican. And just for your information, yes I am a liberal, but I am also a Christian. And I get down on my knees and pray every day, on my own turf, on my own time. One of the things that I pray for, Mr. Brickett, is that people with power will get good sense, and that people with good sense will get power and that the rest of us will be blessed with the patience and the strength to survive the people like you in the meantime!

Jennifer fears she's pregnant after one night with her ex-husband.

The Afternoon Wife
Written by Linda Bloodworth Thomason
Directed by Harry Thomason
Suzanne's first husband Dash Goff visits after writing a book about their marriage.

TOVAH OF BILOXI

Before Charlene married Bill and settled into a life of wedded bliss, she had a weekly appointment with her psychic nutritionist, Tovah of Biloxi (Gloria Cromwell). Suzanne never wasted her time or money on a psychic, preferring to make things happen on her own. Over the years, Tovah frequently predicted that Charlene was about to meet the man she would marry. The candidates included Desi Arnaz Jr., a man she would meet on New Year's Eve who would ask her to dance, and, finally, a diamond in the rough who would have a birthmark on his behind. Tovah also warned Julia to beware of a shoemaker on a red horse. A few days later, a man named Shoemaker sideswiped Julia's car while driving a Mustang. Charlene was convinced, but Julia never became a believer. Tovah also helped Mary Jo when she was reacting to her relationship with J. D. as if he were her unreliable ex-husband, Ted.

Veda
Written by Linda Bloodworth Thomason
Directed by Harry Thomason
Veda Walkman, a new intern from a job placement
  program, makes the other women feel old.

The Conjugal Cottage
Written by Linda Bloodworth Thomason

DRINKING THE INK

There is an old theatrical tale about two English actors who were constantly upstaging each other. One had to give a long monologue downstage, while the other was supposed to sit at a desk upstage and write a letter. The focus of the scene was obviously supposed to be the downstage actor. Night after night, the upstage actor would find some bit of business to get the audience's attention. Finally, after the downstage actor had taken away every prop he thought could be used as a distraction, the upstage actor picked up an inkwell and drank the ink, breaking up the audience once again. Dixie Carter and Delta Burke loved to teasingly accuse each other of "drinking the ink."

Directed by Harry Thomason
When Natalie gets the flu on the same weekend she's supposed to have a conjugal visit with her imprisoned love, Congressman Sharkey, she's forced to send a substitute.

North to Alaska
Written by Linda Bloodworth Thomason
Directed by Harry Thomason
The women visit Alaska to investigate spawning salmon, but find men instead.

YOU'VE BEEN TERMINATED . . .

"Reese's Friend" contains a classic ladies room confrontation.

SHANNON: You don't have to feel threatened by me. I'm not gonna marry Reese or take him away from you. I just want to have a relationship with him for a while. Now if you can handle that, I promise there will be no subterfuge or deceitfulness on my part. Can we be friends?
JULIA: You know, Ms. Gibbs, growing up in the rural part of Georgia, I've been around compost all my life. I've seen it loaded onto wagons and tilled and hoed and spread across fields far and wide. But until today, I must say, I've never seen it tied up and gift wrapped in quite so neat and tidy and pretty a package. Congratulations. You're a very clever girl. But it's still compost. Now if you'll excuse me, I leave you to dig your way out. You do know how to dig, don't you? You just get down on your hands and knees and shovel.
MARY JO: Around the office we call her The Terminator.

Dear Diary
Written by Linda Bloodworth Thomason
Directed by Harry Thomason
Anthony Bouvier visits and Suzanne expects him to
    dispose of a subpoenaed diary that has her weight
    written in it.

Women in Film
Written by Linda Bloodworth Thomason
Directed by Harry Thomason
Suzanne and her staff attempt to convince moviemakers
that they don't have to depict violent acts against
women to have successful films.

From the episode "Dash Goff, the Writer," this photo captures Dash's daydream of four special Southern women. (Left to right) Annie Potts, Dixie Carter, Delta Burke, Jean Smart.

Final Thoughts

"Yesterday in my mind's eye I saw four women standing on a verandah in white gauzy dresses and straw-colored hats. They were having a conversation and it was hot, their hankies tucked in cleavages where eternal trickles of perspiration run from the female breastbone to exotic vacation spots that Southern men often dream about. They were sweet-smelling, coy, cunning, voluptuous, voracious, delicious, pernicious, vexing, and sexing, these earth-sister, rebel mothers, these arousers and carousers, and I was filled with a longing to join them, but like a whim of Scarlet's, they turned suddenly and went inside, shutting me out with the bolt of a latch, and I was left only to pick up an abandoned handkerchief and savor the perfumed shadows of these women, these Southern women, this Suzanne, this Julia, this Mary Jo, and Charlene.

Thanks for the comfort."

—Dash Goff, the writer

Acknowledgments

First and foremost, my thanks to Joe Pittman and the staff at Alyson Books for all their support.

Thanks to Jim Colucci, who is the catalyst for this book's existence.

Much appreciation to the following:

Chanel Anthony, Cheryl Bascom, Fran Bascom, Stacy Bloodworth, Pamela Bowen, Mark Alton Brown, Delta Burke, Camilla Carr, Dixie Carter, Cliff Chally, Eva Charney, Marsha Clark, Paul Clay, Joyce Cohen, Adrienne Crow, Nicole DeMasi, Denny Dillon, Ronnie Claire Edwards, Steve Etheridge, Tom Fitzpatrick, Alice Ghostley, Richard Gilliland, Greg Hernandez, Hal Holbrook, Douglas Jackson, Gary Krasny, Dee LaDuke, Jennifer Levine, Charlie MacNeill, Gerald McRaney, Melanie McMillan, Stacey Million, John Paul Murphy, Maggie Murphy, Pamela Norris, Eileen O'Farrell, Annie Potts, Matt Roush, Jeff Sagansky, Karen Kopins Shaw, Jean Smart, Meshach Taylor, Robert Thomas, Danny Thomason, Harry Thomason, and Ed Zimmerman.

And finally I'd like to give credit to the Southern ladies I grew up with, who gave me such an affinity for *Designing Women* in the first place: My mother and sister, Marilyn Crowe and Kim Crowe; my grandmother, Isla King; my aunts and cousins, Evelyn Jones, Judy King, Gina Simpson, and Ann Marie Jones; and two incredible friends, Alicia Boone and Miriam Boone.